Family Policy, Family Changes

Family Policy, Family Changes: Sweden, Italy and Britain Compared

Patricia Morgan

Civitas: Institute for the Study of Civil Society
London
Registered Charity No. 1085494

First Published March 2006

© The Institute for the Study of Civil Society 2006
77 Great Peter Street
London SW1P 2EZ
Civitas is a registered charity (no. 1085494)
and a company limited by guarantee, registered in
England and Wales (no. 04023541)

email: books@civitas.org.uk

ISBN (10) 1-903386-43-8
ISBN (13) 978-1-903386-43-8

Independence: The Institute for the Study of Civil Society
(Civitas) is a registered educational charity (No. 1085494) and a
company limited by guarantee (No. 04023541). Civitas is financed from a variety of private sources to avoid over-reliance
on any single or small group of donors.

All publications are independently refereed. All the Institute's
publications seek to further its objective of promoting the
advancement of learning. The views expressed are those of the
authors, not of the Institute.

Thanks are due to Catherine Hakim for preparing the tables for
this publication

Typeset by
Civitas

Printed in Great Britain by
St Edmundsbury Press
Bury St Edmunds, Suffolk

Contents

Author

Patricia Morgan is a sociologist specialising in criminology and family policy. She is the author or co-author of a number of books including: *Delinquent Fantasies*, 1978; *Facing Up to Family Income*, 1989; *The Hidden Costs of Childcare*, 1992; *Families in Dreamland*, 1992; *Farewell to the Family*, 1995, *Are Families Affordable?* 1996, *Who Needs Parents?* 1996 and *Adoption and the Care of Children*, 1998, *Marriage-Lite*, 2000 and *Children as Trophies*, 2002. She has contributed chapters to *Full Circle, Family Portraits, The Loss of Virtue, Tried But Untested, Liberating Women From Modern Feminism, Just a Piece of Paper?, Adoption: The Continuing Debate, The Fragmenting Family* and *Margaret Thatcher's Revolution*, as well as articles for periodicals and national newspapers. Her study of the family in New Zealand, *Family Matters: Family Breakdown and its Consequences*, was published by the New Zealand Business Roundtable in 2004. Patricia Morgan is a frequent contributor to television and radio programmes and is presently writing a full-length work on the relationship between capitalism and the family.

Foreword

Nanny state is a fairly universal term of abuse in modern political discourse in Britain. We do not like to be told how to live by politicians, and feel that all lifestyle choices should be permissible in a free society. On the other hand, there is almost universal support for the view that the state should ensure that all citizens enjoy an adequate standard of living, even those who are unable to support themselves because they have made self-destructive choices.

This uncomfortable dichotomy is particularly pronounced in the field of family policy, where personal preference is widely held to be the very last word on the subject. Any politician who is brave enough to point out that some choices are more likely to lead to successful outcomes than others is putting his head on the line. He had better not have any skeletons in his own closet, or they will soon be paraded in the popular press. It is bad form to mention the fact that non-marriage, divorce, out-of-wedlock childbearing, early sexual activity with multiple partners and other 'lifestyle choices' carry risks for both adults and children. Marriage is the M word, to be avoided at all costs.

Family policy, in such circumstances, becomes simply a matter of picking up the pieces, and using taxpayers' money to protect people from the consequences of their own actions. The Blair government's programme to reduce child poverty is a good example of this. The fiscal system is used to transfer money to certain households, whilst the underlying problem—that more children are living in lone-parent households which are likely to experience poverty—is not dealt with.

To a certain extent, the debate is paralysed in Britain by the way in which those who hold opposing viewpoints of what should be done for the family use arguments which are assumed to cancel each other out, as if you have to come down exclusively on one side or the other. Advocates of support for the traditional family argue that Britain has led the Western world in legal changes to facilitate informal relationships. Divorce was made easy, abortion legalised, support for lone parents made more generous and children were secretly provided with the means of sexual promiscuity, in the very early days of the sexual revolution. Hence it should come as no surprise that we tend to top the tables for all the most problematic outcomes, with high levels of divorce, single-parent families, sexually transmitted infections amongst young people and so on.

Champions of alternative lifestyles argue, conversely, that government policy has nothing to do with it. People won't get married just because the government offers them a tax concession. Either they love each other or they don't. If people intend to commit adultery they will do it, without considering the ease with which they can obtain a divorce. Teenagers are going to be sexually active anyway, so we might as well provide them with condoms to limit the damage. According to this view, there is no role for public policy at all, other than to facilitate choices.

In fact, these points of view are not mutually exclusive. In matters as personal as falling in love and getting married, the state will never wield the major influence. People are guided by their deepest feelings, and will want to get married and have children, however difficult these choices may be. However, it is equally eccentric to deny that public policy can have any impact at all. Choices can be made so difficult that for some people, at the margins, they are effectively impossible, or doomed to fail. Poverty is a powerful solvent of relationships, and a fiscal system that offers no support to struggling couples with children will cause the sort of stress that can end a marriage. People who are prepared to work through difficult patches in their marriage suffer frustration when they find that easy, no-fault divorce, largely paid for by the state, allows their spouses to make an exit, regardless of the effect on them or their children.

The purpose of this book is to look at the differences between the state of the family in three developed, Western European countries, and to consider the extent to which public policy goals can explain these differences. Should we praise politicians when families are strong, and blame them when families are weak, or are there other things going on that have to be taken into account?

Patricia Morgan has chosen to compare Britain with Italy, a Southern European country and the home of Roman Catholicism with its traditional family values, and Sweden, a Northern European country where the religious tradition is Protestant (now very weak), and which has been held up as a beacon of progressive, gender-neutral family policy for several decades.

All three countries are members of the European Union, and all have in place the sort of legislation that we take for granted in modern Western societies to permit people to choose their own living arrangements. Divorce is legal, contraception and abortion are available, and the fiscal system is used to support lone-parent families. Of course, there are differences of degree, but, if they want to, the citizens of these three countries could make the same sort of choices. The striking fact—as the chapters and tables that follow reveal—is that they don't.

Italy is still the home of the traditional, extended family based on marriage. Rates of lone-parenthood are extremely low by European standards, especially teenage pregnancies. Cohabitation is so rare as to be almost impossible to measure. Families look after their own members, across and down the generations. Nothing surprising in that, you might say, given the influence of the Roman Catholic church—except that, as far as the Italian government is concerned, family policy is conspicuous by its absence. Not only does the government offer less support to families than almost any other country except Greece, there is evidence that Italians are actively opposed to government involvement in this area. There are too many who can still remember Mussolini's fascistic programmes to use women to breed soldiers.

Sweden is at the other end of the spectrum. There is probably no other country in which the powers of the state have been used so extensively to engineer social outcomes. Sweden was early in the field with far-reaching policies to treat all relationships as equal, with no privileging of marriage, to relieve women of any disadvantages they might experience in the labour market, and to transfer responsibility for the rearing of children from parents to the state. However, things have not turned out completely as planned. Universal childcare proved to be an unattainable goal, given the problems and huge expense of looking after other people's small children, while the gender-neutral employment market turns out to be a somewhat artificial construction—a 'Potemkin workforce' in which thousands of women are paid to stay at home looking after their children on several years of maternity and sick leave.

Britain is in a different situation again. Support for marriage as the basic social institution has been stripped away over a period of 30 years, with the government now claiming to have no policy to encourage one family form at the expense of another. However, the sharp bias that occurs, particularly for low-earners and those on benefits, towards single parents compared with married and two-parent families is a policy of sorts. The fact that Britain tops the league tables of family breakdown in such areas as divorce, lone-parent families and teenage pregnancy cannot be entirely unrelated to a set of policies that, to an extraordinary extent, relieve people of the consequences of their own actions, or at least fail to send out signals to discourage behaviour which is known to have damaging long-term consequences.

What conclusions can be drawn from the mass of information contained in these comparative studies? Perhaps the most obvious one is that there is no one explanation for what happens to families in particular nations. Public policies explain some of it, but not all of it. The other factor—so nebulous and difficult to pin down—is the culture.

Whatever the laws say, and whatever the fiscal system, if you grow up surrounded by people who strongly disapprove of out-of-wedlock childbearing and divorce, you are less likely to become a teenage mother or a divorced parent than if you live surrounded by family and friends who take a very relaxed view of these phenomena. Religious values play an enormously important role. Even in countries where the religious tradition is residual, and many people no longer attend church on a weekly basis, there may be a very strongly internalised desire to avoid disgracing the family and bringing down the neighbourhood by unseemly conduct.

How else can we explain the extremely low levels of single parenthood, especially teenage pregnancy, and the almost invisible amount of cohabitation in Italy? Human nature is pretty much the same everywhere and through time. The sexual urge is not weaker in hot Latin countries—indeed, we have always been led to assume the opposite. But Italian women are highly motivated not to be single mothers, and take the necessary steps. Although abortion is legal in Italy, Table 3 (p. 11) shows that there is much less recourse to it than in other Western countries. For the most part, women try not to get into that difficult situation.

But where does that leave us in terms of public policy? We do not expect the state to encourage us to profess a creed for the sake of social policy outcomes. This is one of those areas in which we definitely feel that the remit of the state does not run. Another such area is the birth rate. We do not want to be told to have children, or not to have them, for the sake of the state. We would regard with equal abhorrence any attempt to impose upon us a Chinese-style one-child family policy, or President Ceaucescu's population-boosting system of rewards for Heroic Mothers of ten or more children. We want the politicians to leave us alone to make these decisions.

However, of all the figures in our tables, there is perhaps none so indicative of the cultural dimension of the state of the family as the average number of children now being born to Western European mothers. Pro-family, Catholic Italy has one of the lowest birth rates in the history of demography. The fertility rate, which needs to be 2.1 children per woman just to replace the population, is down to 1.2, which indicates national extinction in the not unimaginably distant future. Sweden and Britain both have higher fertility rates, and Britain's is unusually high by Western standards, but this is largely achieved as a result of exceptionally high numbers of out-of-wedlock and immigrant births. Nevertheless, the three countries studied in this book, like almost all Western countries, are well below replacement levels of fertility. Whatever political, economic or social explanations might offer themselves, there is no doubt that this is a most important cultural issue, which goes beyond the competence of even the most ambitious politicians and planners.

Patricia Morgan has performed an important service with her North/South comparison of family policy and family outcomes. It is clear that public policy can affect the welfare of the family, but it cannot explain everything that happens. There is a cultural dimension beyond the legal one, so that, even if we were to elect a government which would push through a raft of measures supporting the family, the problems would not disappear overnight. Changing cultures takes longer than changing governments.

Robert Whelan

Introduction

In most modern countries, there has been an assumption that it is inappropriate for the state to seek to influence or shape families, through family policy, and through fiscal policy more generally. In some countries, the argument is that the family is (or is seen as) a *private* sphere of life, separate from the *public* spheres of the workforce, the economy, community activities and public life generally. A popular saying has it that 'An Englishman's home is his castle'. In other countries, family policy is perceived within the context of twentieth-century history, and the eugenic policies and pronatalist policies of totalitarian governments. Again, this leads to a reluctance to admit that governments have any role to play in guiding family trends, by supporting family formation or impeding particular family forms. This is changing with recent developments. Declining birth rates across Europe, and fears about the social and economic consequences of rapidly aging societies, are now slowly breaking down this reluctance to see family policy as just one aspect of the social policies that all European countries organise, explicitly or implicitly.

To some extent, family policy is the policy that has no name. Laws regulating marriage and divorce are universal, although they vary substantially between countries, even within Europe. Such laws obviously do impact on the lifecycle and character of families. Cultural conventions also shape expectations of family life, behaviour, and responses to problems when they occur. This is most obvious in the case of religion.

Devout Catholics do not divorce. In Catholic countries that did not permit divorce, couples learned to live separate lives within the outer shell of an intact marriage and a common household, or even to develop new lives in separate households while technically remaining married. In countries where there is no civil marriage, young couples are perforce obliged to conceptualise their desire to live together within the social and moral framework of the religion's controlling marriage rites. This poses special problems for couples who have grown up

1

within different religious traditions. State support for religious control of family formation and dissolution is family policy by default.

From one perspective, laws and national cultures are inextricably intertwined. However it does make sense to identify the degree of conscious social engineering that operates within a country, as this is tangible, and varies hugely. Sweden, for example, openly and vigorously uses laws, fiscal policy and moral exhortation to promote pronatalist 'gender equality' policies that impact on all aspects of family life, and that are explicitly aimed at *changing* and *forcing* behaviour in particular directions. Southern European countries sometimes have active labour market policies, but do not yet have active family policies similar to Sweden's. However the pace of social change in families is not determined solely by social policies, or their absence. Many other social and economic changes can also have major impacts on family life, notably recessions, the contraceptive revolution and increased longevity.

This book compares family policies and trends in family life in three European countries at a similar level of economic development, with comparable systems of law, and with well developed national political cultures: Sweden, Britain and Italy. The three countries differ sharply in national culture; in social, political and religious characteristics; in family policies; and in patterns of female employment.

This last feature is the easiest to illustrate. The Statistical Office of the European Commission (Eurostat) organises comparisons of labour market trends in all EU member countries every year. The EU Labour Force Survey data summarised in Table 1 (p. 7) show Sweden and Italy to be at opposite extremes regarding female employment, while Britain falls in the middle, close to the EU average. Sweden and Denmark have the highest level of female employment in the EU: three-quarters (72 per cent) of women aged 15-64 years hold jobs of some sort. Italy has fewer women in employment than any other country: 39 per cent, almost half the level in Sweden. Britain is close to the EU average of 56 per cent. These contrasts are not due to the fact that Britain and Sweden have large numbers of women in part-time jobs, unlike Italy. The full-time equivalent (FTE) measure of women's employment favoured by the European Commission takes account of national differences in the incidence of part-time working, yet the measure still shows the same sharp contrasts between Sweden and Italy, as shown in the last column of Table 1.

In other respects, however, official statistics are misleading. Sweden lies closer to the EU average than it looks, because many of the women who hold jobs are not in fact at work at all, but at home full-time on extended parental leave. Recent extensions to parental leave schemes in 2002 mean that women in Sweden can be at home full-time with a small child for 30 months for each successive baby. This amounts to five years for those who have two children. On their return to their jobs, mothers are also entitled to extra days off to care for a sick child, and for other family problems. Whether they return to work full-time or part-time, they can in reality be temporarily at home to a much greater extent than in other EU countries. In contrast, working women in Italy usually work full-time, and are rarely able to take time off work in this way. Studies that focus on the hours actually worked by people in Sweden reveal that, while official statistics indicate almost identical levels of employment among women and men (as shown in Table 1), women's employment is actually one-third lower than men's employment when measured in time spent at work. For example, when the employment rate of mothers with children under seven years old was officially 86 per cent, only 55 per cent were actually at work.[1] This puts female employment in Sweden much closer to the EU average than it appears from EU statistics in Table 1.

The example of Sweden is not unique. In many other European countries, including Britain, rising female employment has been found to be more illusory than real, and an artefact of the way labour market statistics are collected. What has been happening is a *redistribution* of women's employment across a larger number of women, so that more women do paid

3

work, to some extent, at different times of their life.[2] There has been little increase, sometimes a decline, in the proportion of women who work full-time, continuously throughout life, in the same way as men.[3] This warns us against too readily pointing to rising female employment as the cause of changes in fertility and family structure.

In terms of social conditions, the three countries are again reasonably similar and comparable, as shown in Table 2 (pp. 8-10). One key difference is in population size. Britain and Italy are two of the four biggest EU countries with populations of 58-59 million each. In contrast, Sweden is one of the six smallest, with a population well under ten million. The Swedish population is extremely homogenous, in terms of race, religion, language, culture and politics. In contrast, Britain and Italy are large enough to have very diverse and heterogeneous populations, even more so in Britain due to many decades of immigration from outside Europe: the Caribbean, the Indian subcontinent, Africa, Hong Kong and other countries.

Sweden, Britain and Italy are fairly similar in terms of population structure, dependency ratios, life expectancy, marriage rates, median age of students on higher education, women's relative earnings, income distribution and, with some exceptions, ownership of consumer durables. Sweden and Britain are very similar in educational levels, while Italy lags behind on this indicator. However, all three countries now have a preponderance of young women in higher education, with the average age of university students rising across Europe. In contrast, there are sharp differences between the three countries in family formation and family structure. Britain has the highest fertility rate, and Italy has the lowest, even though the three countries are similar in women's average age at childbirth. Births outside marriage are the majority pattern in Sweden, while almost unheard-of in Italy, but are growing fastest in Britain. Teenage pregnancies are most common in Britain but, again, almost unheard-of in Italy. Cohabitation is far less common than births outside marriage might suggest but, again, it is almost unheard-of in Italy, along with divorce. Instead of leaving the parental home to cohabit, young people in Italy continue to live in the parental home while they are in higher education, and up to the time of (delayed) marriage. In Italy, four-fifths of young people aged 16-29 are still living at home, whereas two-fifths of British young people are either married (25 per cent) or else cohabiting (13 per cent) at this age. As a consequence of low divorce rates, and almost no births outside marriage, in Italy only eight per cent of dependent children live in one-parent families compared with 25 per cent in Britain (Table 2, pp. 8-10).

Statistics on legal abortion (Table 3, p. 11) show some interesting country differences. Sweden permitted abortion long before it was legalised in Britain (in the 1960s) and in Italy (in the early 1980s). In Sweden, abortions peaked at 38,000 annually in 1989, and have subsequently declined slowly. It seems clear that abortion continues to be used as one form of birth control in Sweden. This is even more obviously the case in Britain where, again despite easy access to modern contraception, abortions peaked at 200,000 annually in 1998, with a tiny decline since then. In Italy, abortions peaked at 231,000 annually in 1982, and declined steadily over the next two decades, as access to reliable modern contraception reduced unplanned pregnancies.

These trends are echoed in abortion rates, shown in the second part of Table 3. Rates have been declining steadily in Italy since the 27 per cent peak in 1982, as reliable modern contraception became available. In contrast, in Sweden, abortion rates have remained around the 26/27 per cent level since the 1970s. One in four pregnancies is terminated. So abortion remains a fall-back form of contraception in Sweden, even today. Rates in Britain are lower than in Sweden, but are rising slowly rather than falling, despite good access to modern contraception.

One distinctive feature of Sweden is the exceptionally high incidence of suicides, among men and women, although suicides are generally far more common among men. The three countries are similar in terms of people's satisfaction with their

5

financial situation, but Swedes appear to have other sources of discontent with life. Another distinctive feature of the Swedish culture is the relatively high level of trust in the national government, and in justice and the legal system. Trust in the European Union, and in large companies, is highest in Italy, where trust in the national government and political parties is relatively low. However, political parties attract the lowest levels of trust in all three countries.

Overall, social similarities between the three countries are strong enough for meaningful comparisons in the following chapters.

In contrast, the three countries differ dramatically in their social and family policies. These are reviewed in the following three chapters, followed by reviews of family trends and some specific policy consequences. This review of outcomes seeks to differentiate policy levers from the social and economic changes that impact on all European countries, or all modern societies, sooner or later. The final chapter attempts to draw some conclusions about the relative importance of social engineering in contemporary developments.

A brief word on terminology is required. It has become conventional to refer to the one-earner family as 'traditional', even if in reality it is a post-industrial family form, in which one person earns a 'family wage'. Throughout history, both spouses have usually had to work, on farms or in family enterprises, even if, should anyone have to 'go out to work', this was invariably the man. American social scientists have promulgated the label 'traditional' for this form of the family, although the term is elastic enough to cover the common situation where there is one main earner (usually the man) and the family income is supplemented by the wife's (often intermittent and casual) earnings. We use the term in the same sense here.

Table 1
Employment rates and part-time work in the European Union, 2002

	Working-age pop. 15-64 (millions)	Total employment (millions)	Employment rates per cent of working-age population			Part-time workers per cent of all employed		FTE Employment rate
			All	Male	Female	Female	Male	Female
Sweden	5.8	4.4	74	75	72	33	11	63
Denmark	3.5	2.8	76	80	72	30	11	63
Finland	3.5	2.3	68	70	66	18	8	62
Portugal	7.0	5.1	68	76	61	16	7	58
France	37.9	24.9	63	70	57	29	5	51
Austria	5.5	4.0	69	76	63	38	6	51
UK	39.0	29.5	72	78	65	44	9	51
Ireland	2.6	1.8	65	75	55	30	7	47
Luxembourg	0.3	0.3	64	76	52	25	2	46
Germany	54.9	38.9	65	72	59	36	5	46
Belgium	6.8	4.1	60	68	51	37	6	43
Netherlands	10.9	8.3	74	82	66	73	21	42
Greece	6.8	3.9	57	71	43	8	2	41
Spain	27.6	16.3	58	73	44	17	3	40
Italy	38.7	23.9	56	69	42	17	4	39
EU15	250.6	170.4	64	73	56	34	7	47

Notes: The working-age population is people aged 15-64 years. The FTE (full-time equivalent) employment rate assumes that most part-timers work half-time hours, so that two part-time workers are equivalent to one full-time worker. Part-time work is self-defined in the EU Labour Force Survey, with some variation between countries in the upper limit for what are regarded as a part-time hours.
Sources: Labour Force Survey data for 2002 and other sources reported in European Commission, Employment in Europe 2003, 2003.

Table 2
Social indicators for Sweden, Britain and Italy, 1999

	Sweden	UK	Italy
Total population (millions)			
2000	8.9	59.6	57.7
2020 (estimated)	9.1	62.2	56.0
% of population in each age group			
<15	19	19	14
15-64	64	65	68
65+	12	12	14
80+	5	4	4
Age dependency ratio (0-14 and 65+/15-64)			
1998	57	54	47
2010 (estimate)	55	50	54
Old age dependency ratio (65+/15-64)			
1999	27	24	26
2010	28	25	31
Life expectancy at birth – men	77	75	75
– women	82	80	82
Average household size	2.2	2.3	2.7
% of population in households with:			
single parent, dependent/inactive child(ren)	–	4	2
2 adults and dependent/inactive child(ren)	–	35	40
3+ adults and dependent/inactive child(ren)	–	11	14
1 adult, no dependent children	–	10	8
2 adults, no dependent children	–	25	18
3+ adults, no dependent children	–	16	18
Lone parent families as a % of all families	20	9	0.5
% of dependent children living in			
one-parent families (1998)	–	25	8
Average age of leaving parental home – men	–	23	30
– women	–	21	27
% of couples cohabiting	15	9	2
% of live births outside marriage			
1970	19	8	2
1980	40	12	4
1999	55	39	9
Total fertility rate	1.50	1.70	1.21
Average age of women at childbirth	30	28	30
Infant mortality per 1,000 live births			
1970	11	19	30
1999	3	6	5
Teenage pregnancies per 1,000 women aged 15-19	24	45	8
Living arrangements of young people aged 16-29 (1996)			
Cohabiting	–	13	3
Married	–	25	15
Other	–	62	82
Crude marriage rate per 1,000 population	4.0	5.1	4.8

	Sweden	UK	Italy
Crude divorce rate per 1,000 population	2.4	2.7	0.6
% of marriages dissolved by divorce, 1981			
marriage cohort	47	42	8
% of adults who do unpaid childcare, 1996 – men	–	21	15
– women	–	37	37
% of adults who do unpaid eldercare, 1996 – men	–	6	4
– women	–	10	9
Deaths per 100,000 population due to suicide			
and intentional self-harm (1995) – men	20.3	11.3	11.0
– women	8.4	3.0	3.2
Average monthly earnings: women as % of men (1998)	82	72	77
% of men 25-64 with each level of education:			
less than upper secondary	25	17	56
upper secondary	48	54	34
tertiary education	27	29	10
% of women 25-64 with each level of education:			
less than upper secondary	21	24	57
upper secondary	49	51	33
tertiary education	30	25	9
Females per 100 males in tertiary education, 1997	126	107	117
Median age of students in tertiary education, 1997	25	24	–
% of people aged 18-24 having left education with			
low qualifications	7	7	27
% of households owning their accommodation, 1996	58	67	77
% of households owning selected items, 1996:			
telephone	–	94	91
car	72	72	78
colour TV	97	97	97
video recorder	67	82	57
microwave oven	64	74	14
dishwasher	40	23	25
% of persons living in private households in 2000 with:			
mobile phone	71	57	73
personal computer	56	36	36
internet connection at home	61	40	21
% of adults satisfied with their own financial situation	73	69	61
% of households living in houses (not flats) (1995)	57	83	32
% of persons in households receiving (1994)			
social transfers	–	86	50
old age/survivors pensions	–	26	39

Table 2
Social indicators for Sweden, Britain and Italy, 1999 (continued)

	Sweden	UK	Italy
Employment rates of women aged 25-49 (1998)			
all women	–	72	51
women without children	–	79	53
women with 1+ children aged 0-5	–	55	46
Share of income by quintile, 1996			
top quintile	–	42	40
4th quintile	–	23	23
3rd quintile	–	16	17
2nd quintile	–	12	13
bottom quintile	–	7	7
total	–	100	100
Median equivalised income of all persons aged 16+ by level of educational attainment (indexed, total = 100), 1996:			
tertiary education	–	156	162
upper secondary	–	113	121
less than upper secondary	–	86	94
Personal net income from work (indexed, total=100) by age, 1996			
men 16-24	–	45	58
25-49	–	145	112
50-64	–	130	110
women 16-24	–	34	54
25-49	–	80	90
50-64	–	67	88
% of persons 16+ with equivalised income below 60% of median by main activity, 1996:			
employment	–	6	10
unemployment	–	51	44
retired	–	25	13
other inactive	–	30	25
% of persons expressing trust in various institutions:			
European Union	21	20	53
national government	42	36	30
large companies	32	27	41
political parties	17	16	16
trade unions	34	37	28
justice/legal system	53	48	36

Notes: Average earnings of women as % of men's are given for monthly earnings, thus taking no account of the relative incidence of jobs with part-time hours. Dependent children include all children up to the age of 15 plus all those aged 16-24 who are not in the labour force, most of whom are in education.

Sources: Eurostat, *The Social Situation in the European Union,* July 2001, quoting Eurostat statistics and Eurobarometer results. Figures are for 1999 unless otherwise specified.

Teenage pregnancy rates are from Joost van Loon, *Deconstructing the Dutch Utopia,* London: Family Education Trust, 2003.

Table 3
Declared legal abortions and abortion rates

	Sweden	UK	Italy
1960	2,792	0	0
1967	6,388	0	0
1968	10.940	23,600	0
1979	34,709	157,500	0
1980	34,887	168,808	213,310
1982	32,602	171,400	231,008
1990	37,489	197,131	166,046
2001	31,772	197,913	126,164
1960	3	0	0
1967	5	0	0
1968	9	2	0
1979	27	18	0
1980	26	18	25
1982	26	19	27
1990	23	20	23
2001	26	23	19

Note: Abortion rates are calculated as legal abortions as a percentage of conceptions (live births plus legal abortions).
Source: Economic, Social and Demographic Statistics (ESDS) database, Eurostat New Cronos database.

2

Sweden:
Socialist Engineering in Family Policy

1. The Present Situation

The main characteristics of family formation in Sweden in recent decades are:

- declining marriage, more divorce, and rising cohabitation;
- first partnerships are formed at successively younger ages;
- a growth in people living alone;
- steady growth in one-parent families;
- serial monogamy and serial cohabitations are increasingly common;
- the percentage of births outside marriage is rising rapidly, and remains the highest in the EU;
- fertility rates vary sharply, in response to pro-natalist policies;
- suicide rates are among the highest in the EU, exceeded only by Finland.

Family structure

The family of a married couple with one or two children is the most common type in Sweden. In the 1990 census, about 67 per cent of families with children were married-couple-families, and about 15 per cent were unmarried couples. Lone-parent families were around 20 per cent. Of individuals born between 1892 and the mid-1950s, about 85 per cent grew up with both biological parents until 16. Death was the main reason for not growing up with both parents. However, 24 per cent of children born in Sweden during the 1960s and around 29 per cent of those born in 1970-76 no longer lived with both biological parents by age 16.

Living alone has increased: by 1995, 21 per cent of those aged 16-74 were living alone.

There is virtually no adoption in Sweden. The state looks after children who cannot live with their family, since professional educators and carers are preferred to parents. The link with the family of origin is preserved as far as possible.

Marriage

Marriage in Sweden has become a pattern of serial monogamy and serial cohabitations. The marriage rate in Sweden increased in the first half of the twentieth century and up to the 1940s. It began to fall in the late 1940s, and in 1967 a dramatic decline set in. In five years, marriages decreased from 60,000 per year to 40,000. Between 1966 and 1996 the annual marriage rate per 1,000 single women dropped by about a third. The marriage rate shot up in 1989, due to a change in widows' pension rules. (Widows' pensions were abolished to stop women depending on men, but women could still get them if they were born before 1944 and married by 1989.) The median age at marriage has increased by more than six years since the mid-1960s—in 1996, it was 32 for men and 29 for women. In one in ten marriages in the 1950s and one in five in the 1980s, the woman had been married before.

In the 1970s, it seemed that replacement of marriage by cohabitation was taking place and there was no overall decline in partnerships. Indeed, first partnerships were formed at successively younger ages. In 1980, 78 per cent of women aged 20 to 24 in a union cohabited. Of women aged 30-35 this was 28 per cent. Among women born in 1949, about 19 per cent married when entering their first union, while only eight per cent of those born in 1964 married directly.

The propensity for younger women to enter any union increased up to the 1990s, and then levelled off. While women often married after cohabiting for a short time, women in more recent cohorts are now more likely to separate than marry. The dissolution rate for cohabitation is estimated to be two or three times higher than for marriages.[1] While about 20,000 marriages dissolve each year, the number of cohabiting couples separating has increased from about 25,000 in 1981 to 30,000 for 1986-1991. Comparisons of stable cohabiting couples with those who separate reveal little or no socio-economic selection.[2]

The increase of non-marital unions is contributing to 'partnership mobility', in Sweden as elsewhere. These usually last for a short time (shorter than was the case some years ago), and are often followed by successive unions. The Swedes have the highest proportion of women aged 35-39 who have had three or more live-in 'partnerships'.[3] By 1994, about 40 per cent of all new unions involved at least one partner who had been living with someone else before. However, the time between unions means that more people remain unpartnered over the long term. However, cohabitations still last longer than in Britain. It has been calculated that, for women in the age range 20-39 years, dissolved cohabitations had a duration of 29 months, compared with 19 in Britain. Cohabitants that led to marriage had a duration of 48 months, compared with 17 in Britain.

Fewer low-status men are married and more are excluded from family life.

Fertility trends

During the 1930s, Swedish fertility fell to a TPFR of only 1.7 children per woman. In the 1940s, birth rates rose to replacement level. In the 1960s, when birth rates were very high in the Anglophone world, the Swedish rate fell back to just above 1.6. There was a dramatic upturn in the late 1980s and 1990s, as the TPFR rose to 2.14, the highest in Europe. Women had more children and had them earlier, after policy changes allowed women to stay at home on generous allowances during the children's early years. In 1980, the mother (or father) could stay at home with a child for a longer period of time if another child was born within 24 months of the last one. In the 1970s, a woman only had the right to a second period of maternity leave without returning to work if the interval between births did not exceed 12 months—although it had already lengthened with holiday and sick leaves. By the time the period was extended to 30 months, many parents could have two or three children reasonably close together to take advantage of all the benefits and easily remain on paid leave for five years or longer. This meant more births as well as reducing the interval between births, with a big boost in second and subsequent births as the last child reached two years of age. Women in their thirties had a fertility rate higher than those in their twenties. The fertility rate of younger women then started to rise as well, as several cohorts first put off childbearing and then compensated for this, or brought births forward.

Birth rates fell back to a low level by the mid-1990s. The reason may lie partly in cutbacks on wage replacement policies and other adverse economic developments that threatened wages. Also, as in the UK in the 1970s, the very low birth rate may have been due partly to the fact that young women had already brought their birth plans forward and had their children. There was a reduction in the number of couples having third children and a postponement of the birth of the first child. The fall proved to be as temporary as the artificially induced peak, for by 2000 the birth rate had recovered to 1.65— very slightly higher than the UK.[4]

Unwed births

Sweden already had a high illegitimacy rate at the end of the nineteenth century (ten per cent) compared with other European countries, partly because there was a surplus of women, as men migrated, and a very late age at marriage, as people waited to inherit land.

In 1979, 35 per cent of births were out of wedlock compared with less than ten per cent in Britain. Over 50 per cent of births are now outside marriage, overwhelmingly within cohabitations. More first births are within cohabitations than marriages. There appear to be fewer 'single' unwed births than in Britain, where the unwed birth rate is higher than might be expected from the rates of cohabitation. The overall proportion of women who had a child prior to any union was seven per cent in

Sweden in 1995 and there has not been the upward movement seen in Britain. On the other hand, there has been an upward movement in Sweden in first births post first partnership.[5]

There is also the role of cohabitation in driving birth rates down. As elsewhere, cohabiting couples have fewer children than married couples. The formation and disruption of these unstable relationships absorbs time in which children might be conceived and born.

Abortion now deals with nearly 70 per cent of pregnancies out of wedlock in Sweden.

Lone parents

Sweden had one of the highest proportions of lone mothers in Europe in 1979. The increase was greater in the UK in the 1990s, and it has now overtaken Sweden. There is a much lower proportion of young lone mothers in Sweden, with only eight per cent under 25 years old. As elsewhere, lone mothers have fewer children than married mothers (63 per cent have only one child, compared with 37 per cent of married mothers in 1995).

However, more single cohabiting mothers marry than in Britain. France and Britain have the lowest proportion of single, cohabiting mothers who marry, at around one-third, while in Sweden it is 56 per cent within five years, and 70 per cent in Italy.[6]

A high proportion of lone mothers are foreign born, or 20 per cent by 1995. Figures for 1990 show there are more children with lone parents in blue-collar families (25 per cent live with a lone parent) compared with white-collar families (17 per cent). As elsewhere, lone mothers are more likely to be the less educated, low-ability women. Not only do women with higher education have a considerably lower propensity to become lone mothers, but higher earnings before the first child also reduce the risk of entering lone motherhood.[7]

Divorce as a springboard

Overall, the number of individuals experiencing family disruption (from all sources) annually is 140,000-150,000 adults and children. The increasing risks of union dissolution for women born after the late 1950s, in contrast to women born before, is probably due to cohabitations increasing the separation rate. Until the late 1980s, divorce was the main route into lone motherhood.

There was a gradual, continuous increase in divorce from the beginning of the century. The divorce rate increased dramatically in the 1970s following a change in the divorce law in 1974 that allowed divorce on request and at short notice. No reason has to be given, and there is no wait unless there are children (where there is a six month consideration period). Public interference occurs in the case of property and custodial settlements if the couple cannot agree. The annual divorce rate increased immediately by almost 70 per cent, from 8.6 per 1,000 in 1973 to 14.5 per 1,000 marriages in 1974. As elsewhere, after the legal change, the divorce rate dropped somewhat but settled at a far higher level than before. In 1988, the Swedish divorce rate had dropped back to 10.8 per 1,000 married women to rise again by the mid-1990s. Other countries have similar rates: Norway 9.4, Australia 10.8, England and Wales 12.7 in 1989, New Zealand 12.0 in 1990, US 21.0 in 1988.

A factor in the divorce rate is unemployment: as elsewhere, women expect men to be the main breadwinner and reject men who cannot offer much financial support. Amongst children born into marital or cohabiting unions that subsequently became marital unions, there is little difference in the chances of children seeing their parents' relationship break up by their fifth birthday. This is unlike Britain and the US, where children with parents who married from cohabitation are more likely to see their parents split than those born into marriage.

Cohabitation as a springboard

As elsewhere, because cohabitation has such a high dissolution rate compared with marriages, and because cohabitation has become a common way to live, it becomes a leading engine behind the expansion of lone parenthood. According to the cohort study using the Fertility and Family Surveys, 93 per cent of marital unions survive five years after the birth of the first child, compared with 75 per cent of cohabitations (compared with only 48 per cent in Britain).[8] Moreover, previously cohabiting mothers are much less likely to enter a new union compared with those who have been married. Contrary to assumptions about Sweden in the UK, cohabitations have not become equal to marriage in longevity and stability.

2. The Historical Background

These trends paint a picture of increasing social fragmentation. Nonetheless, Sweden has the reputation as the beacon of enlightenment and progress in Europe. One demo-legend has it that Sweden is living proof that cohabitations are as durable as marriages. Another has it that Swedish experience proves that lone parents and their children are more than equal to two-parent families and their children in all outcomes, so long as they get proper support. Sweden 'proves' that young children do better when they go to day care, rather than being reared by mothers at home, and so on. Policy analysts turn to Sweden 'as a widely touted example of modern family policy, a system that recognises the social transformations made necessary by the commitment to gender equality and the full industrialisation of social life... the purest model for a regime of day care, progressive schooling, paid paternal leave... which reconciles the need for human reproduction with the drive for gender equality.'[9] Sweden's welfare state is the model to emulate. The present bias is to classify welfare/fiscal or family policies in such a way as to juxtapose the ideal of the dual-career family who share household duties with the horror of the male breadwinner family and its rigid role segregation. Policies which do not aim to engineer the former are seen as setting out to subjugate women in the latter. The only enlightened policy has become one which gives women equal access to jobs in the labour market, financial independence and high quality subsidised childcare services, so that they never have to choose between a job and having children. This perspective is promoted by Swedish social scientists (as well as policy-makers), who 'have devised several classifications of welfare states that always place the modern Nordic welfare state at the apex of typologies, as the best practice model'.[10] They demand that it must also be exported everywhere else, and it has long been favoured by UK establishment feminists, in and out of government. In 1996, Allan Larsson, Director General of DGV (Directorate General V, responsible for Employment, Industrial Relations and Social Affairs) in the European Commission, complained that women's work-rates in the EU were still lower than men's. He insisted that the days of the male breadwinner had gone and dismissed the 'old social contract' with a division of responsibilities between spouses as 'no longer valid'. Effectively, he demanded that the 'traditional' sexual division of labour must be outlawed, and the Swedish model extended to all in Europe, irrespective of preferences.[11]

Sweden has been cast as the prime example of the 'maximalist welfare state'. Its project is to 'put people's lives straight by defining the content of the good life and controlling the institutional instruments leading to it'. There is even an official list of names from which babies must be named.[12] The justification for such far-reaching intervention and attempts to shape people's fundamental choices in life rests on assumptions that someone knows better than the individuals concerned what the good life is and how it can be achieved. Not least, this has involved the comprehensive political control of family life, where Sweden has made just about the most concerted attempt in history to engineer the freedom of women from child-rearing responsibilities and the demise of the traditional family through economic manipulation, social pressures, and massive public re-education.

> In 1968, Sweden became the first country in the world to frame a government policy of achieving equality between the sexes by changing the role of men as well as that of women. In a statement to the United Nations that year the Swedish government had declared that it was not enough to guarantee women their rights. All legislation and all social policy must support a shift from man-the-breadwinner and woman-the-homemaker to a society of

independent individuals and of partnerships in which all tasks were shared.[13]

In the new century, the remaking of the sexes has been joined by the attempt to equalise 'sexualities'. Books and other media marketed to Swedish schools containing 'unsatisfactory or discriminatory passages concerning homosexuality or bisexuality' are destined for the bonfire. To this end, the National Academy for Education is conducting an extensive review of all schools to determine how principals choose and use textbooks. Schools are now 'empowered' to 'integrate gender equality and sexual orientation issues into their operations and everyday tasks'. As any criticism or objection to the complete normalisation of homosexuality is tacitly defined as psychological abnormality, research is meant to focus upon how 'norms and attitudes make homophobia possible' even where there are 'no statistics or consistent studies which can pinpoint discrimination due to sexual orientation'.[14] Making what may be regarded as offensive statements about homosexuality or homosexuals merits a prison term.

One of the last places in Europe to give anyone the franchise, Sweden is essentially an authoritarian, culturally (and genetically) homogeneous, and small-scale society, with traditions of strong, centralised government, and minimal citizen participation. The cultural and racial homogeneity are largely a function of its small size. As shown in Tables 1 and 2 (pp. 7-10), Sweden is one of the six smallest countries in the EU, whereas Italy and Britain are among the four largest. Historically, little or nothing in the way of intermediate stages or groups developed between a fairly egalitarian and primitive clan-based peasantry and the monarchy. There have been no autonomous trading cities, no merchant classes, no nobility to challenge the state, whose position of power and direct hold over the people has no counterpart elsewhere in Western Europe. This all endowed the expansion of the state and its educative pretensions with a natural legitimacy, and furthered the introduction of collectivist perspectives which demanded strong institutional uniformity and subordinated the rights of the individual to the best interests of the community.[15] Sweden quickly took to twentieth century collectivist notions of the rule of 'expert' elites, possessed of a superior knowledge, of how best people should live.

Added to this, the 'mature industrialism' which took root in the early twentieth century was a 'paradoxical and highly unstable combination of market and command economy'. In 1870 three-quarters of the population were engaged in fishing, farming and forestry, and only nine per cent in manufacturing or crafts. (In Britain, 45 per cent of the labour force were in industry at that time.) Sweden had no coal, but developed hydro-electricity, which led to very rapid economic growth. The 'big factories of mass production were veritable plan and command economies in miniature. Their organisational principles were strictly hierarchic and their top-down chain of command as explicit as in military organisations'.[16] The commanding organisational rationality of big business helped inspire the 'social Fordism' that was repudiated in the USA, but favoured in Germany, the Soviet Union and Sweden, or countries with more corporatist and hierarchic traditions. The Swedish welfare state was to develop along lines which reproduced the centralist and standardised principles of mass manufacturing big industry, the happy factory, or cybernetic Utopia.

Like democracy, Sweden came late to many developments in sexual equality and family law. 'Modernisation' meant the telescoping of the two phases of reform that elsewhere occurred between 1880 and 1900 and then between 1960 and 1975, with Sweden being much later with some and much earlier with other measures. Until 1920, married women had no control over their own earnings, which belonged to the husband. Until 1909, there was no civil marriage. However, illegitimacy as a legal entity was abolished in 1917, not out of radicalism, but because of the ways in which stigmatisation was adding to the problems surrounding children born out of wedlock and their mothers. Liberal divorce laws were introduced in the 1920s and extended in 1974. Homosexuality was decriminalised in 1944. Compulsory sex education was introduced into schools in 1956.

Pronatalism

The impetus behind the family policy measures of the 1930s-1960s was population maintenance, given the low birth rates of the pre-war period. Over a million Swedes left the country between 1860 and 1914, mainly for the USA. There was concern over population shrinkage, as the net fertility rate fell below one in 1927—although it is now alleged that the fertility decline was overstated.[17] The low birth rate resulted, to a not inconsiderable extent, from a low marriage rate and a high proportion of unmarried women. The same was true of the illegitimacy rate. Migration, plus the need to inherit land before marrying, depleted the supply of marriageable men, reduced further by the Great Depression.[18]

Swedish pro-natalism owed much to Alva and Gunnar Myrdal's 1934 book *Crisis in the Population Question*, which provided a pertinent analysis of reproduction in a capitalist society.[19] They argued that, since having children was (irreversibly) voluntary, and based on a living standard criteria, birth rates would probably continue to fall unless something was done to equalise the financial status of those with and without this burden. Those who produced children were massive contributors to the upkeep and perpetuation of the nation, in whom it should invest heavily to secure its future. The Myrdals spoke prophetically of how the long-term development of the proposed welfare state, which would include provisions for the aged as well as children, might add dramatically to anti-family pressures which discouraged the birth of children by passing massive resources and influence to the elderly.

Old age pensions stripped children of economic value and reversed the incentives structure. It had become rational for people to avoid the expense of children, while hoping that others will be foolish enough to rear the children who would later pay for everyone's retirement. Young people were required to support the retired and the needy through the welfare system as well as the children to whom they gave life. Consequently, they reduced the number of children because it was the only factor over which they had any control. In contrast to the neo-Malthusians, who saw increased living standards as the result of population decline, it was argued that an aging population would mean more medical and welfare costs falling on a decreasing number of economically active people, as the economy contracted with falling demand and less capital formation. Also to consider as the aged inherited the earth, was the prospect of the debilitating and stultifying power of the elders.

The Myrdals wrested the population question away from conservatives and nationalists and turned it towards the service of socialist goals. 'With exquisite timing, the Myrdals offered the [Social Democratic] party a wildly popular, politically effective, scientifically justified response to what had been seen as an unsolvable problem, and they went on to reshape their nation.'[20] As transformers of the Swedish state, their achievement knows few parallels. They epitomised the collectivist social engineer who manages society according to scientific principles for constructive ends. To the elite expert, existing social life was just 'the illogical result of human choices; at any moment we could decide whether to maintain or change it'. Distinctions 'between facts and values were blurred and jargon became a convenient cover for political goals'.[21] As the Myrdals pursued 'social revolution they foreclosed other options and possibilities and so served as progenitors of the post-family welfare state'.[22]

Calling for a 'forced march into modernity as the only hope for families and children', the Myrdals linked voluntary parenthood, sex education and birth control to the feminist theme of women's full engagement in the labour market and thence to the nationalist desire to ensure population stability. Gunnar Myrdal himself had an authentic desire to increase the birth rate, while Alva was more committed to a gender role revolution, achieved through the use of the population issue as a political tool. Both saw the radical-conservative consensus on the population question as the crowbar for the socialisation of Sweden. Only sex would be left to individuals and the hope was that this would secure enough children to fund the whole enterprise.

Importing the revolution

Before it erupted in the West in the late 1960s, the doctrinal base for sexual liberation and gender equality was laid in Sweden by the same body of feminists influential in the early Soviet Union's programme for sexual freedom. Both communists and social democrats, supported by Alva and Gunnar Myrdal, were part of the interwar functionist movement which attacked the garden cities of England and the workers' apartments of Europe as incompatible with women's employment and freedom from 'household drudgery'. Even if it was 'inspired by socialist sympathies', the low-cost housing built in Western Europe between the two world wars did not have as its goal the remodelling of the family or society, but the amelioration of an ugly by-product of capitalism—the squalid slums of the industrial cities. 'The [limited] goals were space, hygiene and fresh air.'[23] Embracing Le Corbusier's 'machine for living', the Myrdals and other policy-makers wanted the 'collective house' to house the new people, with the women at work, the children in care centres, and social workers and educators overseeing everything. The family dilemma in Western society would be resolved—on Friedrich Engels's terms—by the development of more 'efficient' forms of child-rearing better suited to the industrial age. Daycare and summer camps would be less expensive than supporting the antiquated and maladaptive family where children were exposed to a damaging psychological atmosphere. The 'falsely individualistic desire' of parents for the 'freedom' to raise their own children was unhealthy. It was 'based on a sadistic disposition to extend this "freedom" to an unbound and uncontrolled right to dominate others'.[24] In the collective nursery, small children would be cared for twenty fours hours a day by highly trained personnel, in hygienic conditions, with pedagogically correct playthings. (This is not far from the 'children's centres' envisaged by the Blair government as an outcrop of the Sure Start programme, where children can stay from early morning to evening while the parent works.)

In these conditions, women would have more children. If there were not enough jobs, then public works, sound economic planning and a growing economy would create enough for everybody. The blueprint was for communities where 'property was owned jointly, work was shared, food was prepared in common, and children brought up together'. Men and women would then 'be equal and independent, and sexual morality... not defined by legal norms'. The 'aim was to break the bonds that private property and conventional family ties imposed on the development of the individual in a free society'. Collective housekeeping was 'not just a convenience for women but... part of the structure necessary for creating socialist relationships'.[25]

In turn, reducing the time together in the home would undermine the influence of parents on their children's development.

For the reformers, a rational allocation of resources meant benefits in kind, or as 'social consumption' rather than cash. Otherwise, family allowances might be added to the main family budget, rather than spent directly on the children. Society must assume most of the child support function, financed by taxes on the whole population, and dispense free meals, free medical care, clothing, infant care, 'modern, hygienic furniture' and so forth. Such collectivised programmes would prove cheaper, more effective and adequate in meeting need, than individual choice, and allowed for social transformation through the removal of independent action. Ordinary people lacked the sense to know what was good for them. Consumption, the last economic function left to the family, must be socialised.[26]

The Myrdals dominated political and social discourse in the interwar period to the extent that to engage in sexual intercourse was 'to Myrdal' and a sofa was a 'Myrdal couch'.[27] But the reform programme, with its daycare for children, went beyond the confines of Social Democratic policy-making and opinion in the 1930s and 1940s. Actual family policy reforms included free maternity care in public clinics, rent rebates according to family size, child tax allowances, marriage loans and employment protection for mothers. In 1948, family allowances for all children were introduced to replace child tax allowances. Many of these measures existed in the UK, such as maternity care and child health measures; family allowances were introduced in Britain in 1943, and ran alongside child tax allowances until 1979. Policies supporting full employment through Keynesian manipulation were also common pro-family measures throughout the post-war Anglophone world—as in Australia and New Zealand. However, in Sweden, a more explicit pro-natalist population policy, allied with Keynesian counter-cyclical public expenditure policies, specifically legitimated the expansion of the welfare state. The goal was to increase fertility by 25 per cent, and to improve the quality of the next generation by improvements in child welfare. As elsewhere, pronatalism and the preservation of the nation were not then deemed to be racist or fascist.

From the time that Swedish welfare programmes were first constructed in the 1930s, there was much concern, not just with horizontal equity, but with the vertical redistribution that was eschewed in the Anglophile world. The welfare state was seen as an instrument of equality, rather than simply a device for easing pressure at various points in the life cycle.

Social engineering: the feminist paradise

By the 1960s, the goal of achieving a real redistribution of wealth, or even a reduction in income differentials through full employment and measures for non-earning members of society, seemed even further off. Inequalities had widened. Opportunities for advancement went to those who already had opportunities, while grants, loans and tax breaks for enterprise increased the wealth gaps. Victims of a 'new poverty' were principally those with children, and especially lone parents, big families and immigrants. What was 'redistributed' back to parents was little compared with what they paid in taxes to finance benefits and services (plus the administrative costs) that went primarily to others—especially the retired. By 1958, pensioners were receiving a higher income than members of families with dependent children.

Sweden saw much the same upsurge in crime in the 1960s as other Western countries; lower than the UK, France and the Netherlands, but higher than Germany, Italy and Austria.

The contemporary counter-cultural upheaval in the Anglophone world was re-cycling feminist and socialist perspectives from the late nineteenth and early twentieth century— perspectives that already had greater prominence and success in Sweden.

The debate on class equality was joined by a re-vamped gender debate, dominated by progressive sociologists and psychologists. By now, 'social parenting' was a definite prerequisite for a liberated sexuality which was incompatible with child-rearing based in marriage. With reformers preoccupied with class and gender equality, the aim was a society where individuals, undefined by sex, marriage, or parenthood, were never dependent upon anybody else, and in continuous fulltime work regardless of marital and parental status. The Erlander Report,[28] adopted by the Swedish Social Democrats in 1964, and supported by communists and liberals, insisted that government powers over industry and education were to be used to eliminate sex discrimination, sex-determined choices of occupation, and to set up childcare. In comparison, moves to diminish the conflict between work and family merely perpetuated the idea that women's task was homemaking and the care of children. There must be no 'right to choose' between home and career at any time in life, and men and women must unavoidably have the same obligations. People did not know their own minds; they were just 'culturally conditioned' and frozen into an impoverishing mould.

With the goals being the sameness of contribution and equality of outcome, attained by the break-up of the sexual division of labour in the home, and equal opportunities and affirmative action policies outside, the Social Democrats' women's organisation got them incorporated into the party's 'Programme for Equality', adopted in 1969. It involved a sleight of hand and was never really debated publicly. The programme was presented as having something for everyone, so the inclusion of women, or the social engineering of the new women and new men, remained largely implicit.

Everybody working

The reduction of poverty was sought through wages policy, in the context of the pursuit of full employment. This is not the 'living wage' policy pursued by governments and trade unions in Anglophile countries from the mid-nineteenth to the mid-twentieth century—the aim of ensuring male breadwinners an income sufficient to keep a smallish family at a modest but adequate living standard. Instead, with the aim of keeping all parents in employment there had to be the same remuneration, as well as employment and family work patterns, for both sexes. Twinned with the goal of reducing gender inequality was one of equalising income between family types. This itself was part of ensuring equality across classes. Labour shortages dictated that all women had to work, to avoid the need for immigration, with its consequent social problems. (Other countries, like the UK and Germany, imported labour from less developed countries.)

To engineer these outcomes, unmarried and married couples were treated alike in respect of tax assessment, housing allowances and child benefit. Individual taxation of spouses replaced joint taxation in 1971. The principle of family equity as applied fiscally—that income be taxed in proportion to the numbers dependent upon it—was annulled on the grounds that nobody should rely on anybody else, and children were preferably reared by the state.

'Social democrats sacrificed one of their most hallowed principles... in order to force a tax on the imputed income of the homemaker and to drive all mothers into the marketplace.'[29] As an added penalty on mutual support, a family with only one earner received a lower housing benefit than one with the same net income earned by two. Housing benefit is paid per person. Since 1995, a 'partner' with no income is not entitled to any housing benefit, so that the couple will have an income limit under a half that allowed a lone parent.

With very high progressive taxation, it became impossible (as intended) to live on one wage, and more economically advantageous for the woman to work, than for the man to work longer hours or get more remunerative work. The resultant high female work-rates have been interpreted as reflecting women's preferences for paid work over family work and for financial independence over interdependence with a spouse.

All in the crèche

To put further pressure on both parents to work, subsidised day-care became the main form of 'help' for families. The state took on, and socialised, many family responsibilities to a degree unseen outside of the Soviet bloc, not least the rearing of children in crèches (ideally) or with minders.[30] To rid the world of sex roles was not only an educational endeavour, it also demanded intervention into personality development and attitudes. Given assumptions about the overwhelming role of early experience, pre-school care offered the opportunity to combat early differences in the personalities of the sexes while parents were occupied at work.[31]

Parenthood was separated from marriage, and the word 'custodian' adopted to designate the person immediately responsible for a child. These custodians are acting for the state which 'is not only the supervisor but also the agency which creates the conditions under which mothers and fathers are acting as parent'.[32] An 'aspect of the integration of paid work and parenting is that in child development and education, parental work must be shared with paid professionals. The professionals do their job as paid work, which means that the rules of their working organisations and labour unions set certain limits on parental influence'.[33]

While parents are expected to go to meetings at daycare centres 'to be informed about the situation and the plans for the daycare centres and the children... Parents are generally not supposed to interfere... In school there are even fewer possibilities to influence the way children are taken care of and the education they get. All in all, there is a loss of parental control over the development of the child.'[34]

The public care system, introduced in the 1960s, covers about 50 per cent of children aged six or under (school starts at seven years of age), and about a third of under-threes are cared for in municipal nurseries or by salaried childminders. Fees at day-care centres are heavily subsidised and amount to around 10-15 per cent of the actual costs. They are determined separately in each municipality. A place in a centre cost about two thirds of the average gross wage by the mid-1980s. Lone parents have generally had priority for places, even if they do not work, at reduced rates. The proportion of children in public daycare is higher for lone- than for two-parent families. By the 1990s, almost half of children with two parents used municipal childcare compared with three-quarters of children with lone parents.

Childminders have to look after at least four children full-time, or eight to ten part-time, to get their salary. One reason so many children still go to childminders is that many municipalities only admit children needing full-time care to nurseries, since nursery places are too costly to use part-time. Another reason is the need to meet targets for daycare coverage, which has meant registering unofficial or 'black day mothers' as salaried childminders (many are women trying to finance the rearing of their own children by taking in other people's at a knock-down price). The local authority hires the mother by inserting a subsidy into the system that helps her to pay her taxes while staying at home. Unlike the nurseries, childminders only have to meet minimal standards to be approved.

There has been some conflict between local authorities and the central government over the expansion of institutional daycare, and in some municipalities by the 1990s lone mothers only had priority for places if they were employed. The availability of 'socialised' childcare has been patchy compared with both aspirations and proclamations, not least because it turned out to be the most unimaginably expensive and inefficient way to look after children. The necessary resources, not least in terms of trained personnel, were simply not there. Although daycare became the largest single item on many municipal budgets by the 1970s, and the construction and staffing of a network of care facilities proceeded apace (the number of nursery places increased ten-fold between 1970 and 1980), the timescale for national coverage of all pre-school children was continually revised.

There are objections to the removal of childcare from unemployed parents on the grounds that this violates the UN Convention on the Rights of the Child. It is seen as discriminatory that children are denied something as fundamental to their development and freedom as childcare purely because of their parents' work status.[35]

The benefits system

Benefits in kind, or as 'social consumption' rather than cash, allowed for social transformation through the removal of independent action and choice. Applications to deal with child poverty by paying municipal family allowances (a tradition in the Germanic and Scandinavian world) to 'unfavoured' families (i.e. those without a working mother), which might in part compensate for the daycare subsidies they had paid for but did not use, were disallowed.

A strict 'availability for work' test has been applied to the unemployed, with no allowance for lone parents or anyone's childcare responsibilities. (In Britain, there are relatively weak work tests, so a lone parent does not have to work until the youngest child is 16.) In Sweden, parenting is allowed for in the employment programme, but it is a break from a career. Work is not supposed to be fitted around a family. Instead, allowances are made for families in employment.

Public transfers are strongly income-redistributive, and many services are heavily subsidised or free of charge. Transfer and insurance schemes are usually universal. Unlike other redistributist welfare regimes, real or aspirational, policy has generally avoided means-testing, or has not focused on it. The few means-tested benefits, like the housing allowance and social benefit, have not been a big aspect of the welfare system and, unlike elsewhere, do not have so much impact on labour supply. There is a universal child allowance, with a supplement for the second child. Child allowances have largely kept pace with retail prices, adding about five per cent per child to the gross earnings of the industrial worker. In 1996 the amount was reduced. By 1997 the level of family allowance and the supplement for the second child were restored. At the time of writing the family allowance is €105 a month, with a €28 supplement for the third child, €84 for the fourth child, and €105 for each subsequent child.

However, payments in kind and, particularly, income replacement during maternity/parental leave account for more than 65 per cent of all family benefits in countries like Denmark and Sweden. Cash family benefits account for only 30 per cent of all child/family benefits, compared to well over 50 per cent in Italy and the UK.[36]

Parental leave

Parental leave income replacement programmes were introduced in 1974. In 1989, the duration of paid leave became 60 weeks. Payment during leave was 75 per cent to 90 per cent of earnings for 48 weeks, and then a minimum guaranteed amount. The rate for the first 48 weeks fell to 85 per cent in 1995 and to 75 per cent in 1996; to return to 80 per cent in 1998. The 'eligibility interval' also expanded, so that if a woman bears the next child within this interval, she is entitled to exactly the same benefits that she received for her previous birth. The interval rose from 12 months in 1974-77 to 30 months in 1986. In the 1970s, a woman had only the right to a second period of maternity leave without returning to work if the interval between births did not exceed 12 months—although it had already lengthened with holiday and sick leaves. With the period extended to 30 months, many parents could have two or three children reasonably close together to take advantage of all the benefits and easily remain on paid leave for five years or longer.

Since after-tax income does not allow one parent to stay home with children, the economy of the family is very much dependent upon the woman having a paid job—the insurance money from parental leave is aimed at refunding the income lost from paid work, not for having children to look after.

In 1995, one month of Swedish parental leave was earmarked for the father, since mothers were using most days (90 per cent or more in 1993-96). Despite all the propaganda and various pressures, men do not usually take parental leave, and role reversal is very rare. Men's use of parental leave is also low elsewhere: one per cent in Norway, two per cent in Denmark, three per cent in Iceland, with a maximum of 13 per cent in Finland. Most mothers prefer not to share the care of a newborn with the father.[37] So men are being made to 'care', like it or not. Three-quarters of mothers and fathers were opposed to compelling men to take parental leave.[38] The new rule made little impact. By the late 1990s, fathers were still taking only 11 per cent of leave days, and half took none at all. Most of those men who took it worked in the public sector and had wives in high-status jobs. Despite all the enthusiasm for Swedish role reversal in the UK press, it is not a reality even in Sweden, only rhetoric.[39] The work environment is hostile to workers in key posts or with special skills taking so much time off.

The parental leave system is used by more two-parent families than lone parents. In 1993, this was 93 per cent compared to 55 per cent. Until the child is 12 years old, parents are allowed to take time off work to stay at home when the child is ill, at the rate of 75 per cent of earnings, up to a maximum of 60 days per year.

In January 2002, the parental leave scheme was changed, to add a second daddy-month, on top of the existing allowance rather than at the expense of the mother's allowance. In January 2003, the income guarantee level was raised again. The objectives of the reform were to enhance an early and close contact between father and child; to reduce employer discrimination against fathers and mothers on parental leave; and to promote a less unequal division of household and childcare responsibilities in order to achieve less unequal labour market outcomes. It was believed that increasing daddy-months in parental leave would have the long-term effect of reducing occupational segregation and the pay gap. Evaluation studies show a slightly increased fathers' use of parental leave, although this still remains very low, at 17 per cent of all the leave available to couples—a very slow increase from seven per cent in 1987. However the biggest effect was to persuade most fathers to take at least a few days' leave, rather than none at all. Before the change, over half of all new fathers took no daddy-leave days off work. After the change, total non-use was reduced to 20 per cent. One-third of new fathers took one month off work. Surprisingly, the change had no impact at all on fathers' propensity to take time off to care for a sick child. Many fathers simply used the extra leave to top up their summer holiday and Christmas holiday allowances. Peak times for the use of daddy-leave days are in August and late December, especially as they can be taken at any time up to the child's eighth birthday.[40] Anecdotal evidence suggests that fishing trips are more popular than changing nappies. Undeterred, the government is considering whether to force fathers to take one-third of all parental leave. However, it is reluctant to push through the change, because it could be sufficiently unpopular to be a vote-loser.

Double income for lone mothers?

A problem with these arrangements is that equal pay and employment for men and women results in a living standard based on double incomes. This defeats the aim of equalising outcomes for lone- and two-parent families—since lone mothers only have one income to rely on. So the state makes a 'child maintenance advance' for lone parents, paid by the Social Insurance Office, which tries to claim a proportion of it back from the absent parent. The payment is additional and above the rate of child allowance.[41] The government recovers about a third of the expenditure from fathers—something that became a matter of some debate in the 1990s. There are no such guaranteed payments in Britain, although they are an aim of the lone-parent lobby (and were proposed by the Finer Committee[42]). In Sweden, as in Britain, mothers on public assistance do not benefit from maintenance unless the payment lifts income above the benefit line. Giving lone mothers double incomes means that couples on one wage are going to be worse off than lone parents. With two children and average earnings, a lone parent in Sweden in 1996 was 35 per cent better off than a one-earner couple on average earnings. However, on a half of average earnings, the lone parent would have 92 per cent of the net income of the couple.

How much has it cost?

In order for the state to provide services socially that otherwise would be privately provided in the family, many ordinary, everyday personal services must be reckoned in monetary terms, tax revenues raised to finance them, and complex rules and conditions imposed to limit undesirable side effects.[43] In 1960, 'real social expenditure' in Sweden was around 16 per cent of GDP, just above average for OECD countries. In 1981, 'real social expenditure' accounted for almost 34 per cent of GDP, exceeded only by Belgium and the Netherlands. In the years 1975-1981, real social welfare spending increased four times as fast as the economy as a whole, and twice as fast as the OECD average in that period. Sweden's general government outlay as a share of national output amounted to 59 per cent by 2003—a rise of nearly 28 per cent from 1960, with an estimated restrictive effect on output of 390 per cent.[44] By the late 1970s, a skilled worker on the average wage paid 50 per cent income in taxation—down to over 40 per cent in the late 1980s (34.2 per cent in 2000/2001 at an average production wage and 42.6 at twice average earnings).[45] Employers still pay around 40 per cent payroll tax for social welfare. The Swedish tax take has been overtaken by Denmark, Germany, Belgium and the Netherlands in the twenty-first century (if the employer's social security liability is excluded).[46] In practice, only a limited portion of what is paid as tax is redistributed between different groups; the 'greater part really goes into a whirligig which transforms our money into political power over ourselves'.[47] By 1990, the public sector accounted for 37 per cent of the labour force—more than manufacturing industry (20 per cent). Similarly, in Denmark the number of female homemakers declined by 579,000 between 1960 and 1982, as the number of employees in the public sector grew by 532,000, with most of the growth in daycare, elder care, hospitals and schools.[48]

The Swedish system has been characterised as a system where the private sector maintains nominal control over its capital and labour, but the returns on the factors of production are so heavily circumscribed by regulations, directives and taxes that the state, or public sector, ends up effectively controlling them. A 'sham form of mixed economy', it has traditionally been associated with Fascist regimes. This kind of *gelenkte Wirtschaft* (joined up) economy is popular with politicians and bureaucrats because all sectors of society are forced to keep on good terms with the state and its functionaries if they are to remain in business. Such 'Third Way' economies seem to be capable of generating good growth in their early years, as GNP is boosted by the public spending component. They eventually slow down and seize up as investors become aware of the ways in which their returns are being expropriated. All the regulations and controls create inefficiencies that, in turn, lead to more controls, until a point is reached when deregulation becomes necessary if the system is to survive.[49]

A perennial justification for putting all women into the labour force and into more productive work than childrearing is that this will make everyone richer: 'To the extent that female participation remains at depressed levels due to market failures and policy distortions, (*sic*) removing these could lead to higher levels of welfare.'[50] In Sweden, between the mid-1970s to mid-1990s, disposable income increased by around 18 per cent, reckoned per consumption unit after taxes and transfers. Most of the increase is attributable to the roughly equivalent rise in employment rates among women, with rising incomes concentrated among joint households, particularly middle-aged (30-64 years) and childless households.[51] But there was little growth in real incomes for full-time employees (three per cent). People have simply been made to put more labour onto the market. They expend double the effort and are disabled from cooperating to exploit any division of labour or to specialise. If Swedish women take care of each other's children in exchange for others taking care of theirs, how much additional output can come out of this?

3. Have the Policies Worked?

Has Sweden solved the 'lone parent' problem?

In the UK, as throughout the Anglophone world, lone parents tend to rely heavily on public assistance, to be dispro-portionately economically inactive and to have a high propor-tion of their number under, at, or around the poverty threshold. It is repeatedly claimed that lone parents could be self-supporting if only they had the childcare and the jobs. Only lack of these is stopping them from working full-time, which they are supposedly desperate to do. Indeed, some have gone so far as to claim that the state could make a profit from providing childcare, which will get mothers off benefits and paying taxes instead.

Sweden has done more or less everything every good progressive says it should do to put mothers into work, abolish lone-parent poverty, rid them of dependence on the state or means-tested subsidies and ensure equal outcomes for different 'family forms'. It allows us to test the hypothesis that it is marriage and children that make women poor. In this view, lone parents are not at risk of poverty because one person has all the parental functions. Instead, it is the family and its division of labour that are the main cause of the high poverty among lone mothers. Their plight mirrors and concentrates women's difficulties as an economically disadvantaged group compared with husbands and fathers. Society could easily arrange to pass babies onto a child-rearing agency. This would get rid of women's caring penalty (that is, all the money lost while looking after others), and enable them to accumulate greater income for themselves.[52]

So has the Swedish model lived up to expectations?

The growth in poverty

Compared with their position elsewhere, Swedish policy on lone parents is a success, since their poverty rate is low. In 1982-87, there was no significant difference between lone and couple-mothers in the prevalence of poverty. At this time, 23 per cent of children in lone-parent families lived in homes with below 40 per cent of the adjusted median income. This drops to two per cent when post-tax and transfer incomes are compared. For children in two-parent families this is 1.5 per cent. In the USA, at the same time, 54 per cent of children with lone parents experienced both low post-tax and transfer incomes.

In Sweden and Norway, lone-parent families had 85 per cent of the adjusted (equivalised) disposable income of members of two-parent families in 1995. In Germany, France and the UK it was between 65 and 76 per cent, and below 60 per cent in Australia, Canada and the US. The difference was due to the universal child allowance, an advanced maintenance benefit, subsidised childcare and parental leave insurance. A strong contributory factor for lone parents' low incomes in other countries is that means-tested benefits serve as negative incentives for employment, or (for those in employment) for moving from part-time to full-time work, or otherwise increasing earnings.

However, a large number of Swedish lone mothers have incomes only slightly above the poverty line. In the 1990s, Sweden saw a rise in poverty rates for lone mothers from four to ten per cent. Poverty has increased for both lone and couple-mothers, but from 1988-91 and up to 1995, lone mothers were more likely to be poor than couple-mothers, their situation having deteriorated after the late 1980s, both relatively and absolutely.

On the one hand, equivalent disposable income in the early 1990s developed more unfavourably for couples, compared with lone parents, since transfer payments cushioned the decrease in market income more for lone than couple-families. However, the mid-1990s saw general cuts in the benefit system, with rising costs for housing, childcare, health and social insurance. This affects those who are net receivers of transfers, principally lone mothers, even if they are still better protected by the benefits system.

On all indicators of economic security, the percentage of children living with lone parents who experienced insecurity was roughly double that of children with two parents in 1995. Various groups were analysed in a report from the National Board of Welfare[53] on the situation of vulnerable groups in relation to having three or more problems concerning housework, employment or earning a living. Among lone mothers aged 25-64, 27 per cent had three or more problems compared with ten per cent for the whole population. Among lone mothers aged 25-34, 36 per cent had three or more problems, rising to 51 per cent when they lived in big cities. Families generally had more economic problems. Overall, 28 per cent of all children aged 0-15, compared with 17 per cent of the population as a whole, lived in families which had difficulty in meeting expenses for food, housing and other basic requirements during the year preceding the interview.[54]

While there was some recovery by the end of the century, poverty rates for lone mothers without work were still 34.2 per cent in 2000, and 5.6 per cent for those working. For two-parent families, the rates were 13.7 per cent where there was no worker, and 1.6 per cent where there were two—but a higher rate of 8.2 per cent where there was one worker.[55] This testifies to both the precarious position of lone parents in the labour market, and the lack of support for one-wage, two-parent families, compared with the big subsidies going to lone working parents.

Declining employment

In 1979, Swedish lone mothers were more likely than couple-mothers to be employed: 83.5 and 79.3 per cent respectively. In the mid-1980s, employment was 85 per cent for both groups. Reversal happened in the 1990s. In 1994, the participation of lone mothers in the labour market was 70 per cent and for married and cohabiting women it was 79 per cent. Similarly in Britain, the proportion of lone mothers who were employed declined to 42 per cent compared with 65 per cent of couple-mothers in 1992-5. Long-term unemployment increased for both lone and couple-mothers, but rates of unemployment increased among lone mothers from 4.8 in 1979 to 11.9 in 1992-5. Lone mothers have a three-times higher risk of unemployment than couple-mothers.[56] The proportion economically inactive was also higher in lone than couple-mothers; peaking in 1992-5 with 8.3 of lone mothers and 3.6 of couple-mothers. Between 1990-95, the proportion of children living with two gainfully employed parents, married or cohabiting, decreased from 84 to 67 per cent. The proportion of children living with a lone mother who was employed declined from 72 to 58 per cent between 1985 and 1995, and with a full-time employed lone mother from 36 to 31 per cent.

Lone mothers are part of a trend whereby the proportion of people finding themselves outside the labour market increased over the 1980s and 1990s, despite a shortage of manpower. The risk of unemployment falls with rising education and lone mothers have poorer educational levels compared with married mothers. However, even with the same educational attainment, the 'risk' of unemployment is double for lone mothers. Lone mothers may have a weaker bargaining position in the labour market,[57] and face more discrimination, even in Sweden. They consider themselves to have less secure jobs than married mothers, and report less understanding attitudes towards their parenting role if, for example, they have to stay at home with a sick child. Sympathetic employment in the private sector is precarious, and the limits to public sector employment have been reached.

An egalitarian wage structure and taxes, rather than the welfare state's negative effects on work, savings and investment via means-tested benefits (as in the UK, Australia and New Zealand), undermine Swedish women's incentives to work more hours, or to upgrade and invest in skills. Scandinavian public employment offers good pay and security, but imposes a growing tax burden. With high rates of productivity growth the system can be sustained; when productivity or private investment is sluggish, severe cost problems emerge. Sweden in the mid-80s faced declining fiscal capacity combined with rising pressures on public job creation and/or income maintenance. Wage differentials have since grown, and adjustments to benefit entitlements have aimed to reduce disincentives and high absenteeism. Replacement rates for sickness, parental leave and unemployment benefits have been trimmed, and the second tier pension system overhauled. Pension contribution years have been extended and benefits are now more tightly related to contributions.

The fiction of self-sufficiency

Tendencies to decreasing workforce participation levels, decreasing disposable income, and vulnerability to poverty as well as welfare dependency, suggest that the position of lone parents is precarious in Sweden, as elsewhere, and raise questions about the capacity of Swedish policies concerning lone parents to make them self-supporting, if not affluent.

Making lone parents 'self sufficient', let alone economically equal to couples, means that their incomes are maintained with immense subsidies from the state. Couples are positive or net contributors to the public purse; lone parents are massive recipients of transfers. Transfers ensure that the adjusted income for lone mothers is approximately 85-87 per cent of the corresponding income for intact two-parent families. If no income redistribution occurred it would be 55 per cent, given the same labour market participation. All in all, adjusted disposable income is higher than the factor income for lone mothers, and substantially lower for intact families with children (who are making the big transfer to lone mothers). By 1985, public transfers of different kinds accounted for 40 per cent of the overall net income of lone mothers, compared with eight per cent for families with two earners. Even so, transfers only covered two-thirds of the gap between divorced mothers and intact families. By 1993, in more difficult times, lone-parent families received 55 per cent of their gross income from the market, and 45 per cent as transfer payments. The proportions for couples with children were 79 per cent and 21 per cent respectively.

Dependence on transfers makes lone parents vulnerable to cuts in programmes. The recession during the early 1990s resulted in frozen or reduced levels of state benefits, and a stricter policy towards social welfare assistance. As workers, lone parents are one of the first groups to be affected by adverse macroeconomic developments, even if they have low levels of poverty in Sweden compared with other countries. The decline in their fortunes was detectable by the end of the 1980s as their position in the labour market deteriorated, and they faced decreasing real wages and rising childcare costs, as childcare institutions were forced to reduce staff and raise costs. This has had a knock-on effect, since universal benefits, for sickness, unemployment, etc., are based on labour market performance.

Growing welfare dependency

The proportion of households that are dependent on social assistance, whether at any time or for long periods, has grown, particularly for lone mothers.[58] Over time, they are six times more likely to receive social welfare and twice as likely to get unemployment benefits. In 1970, 25 per cent of lone mothers received social assistance, and by 1995, this was more than every third lone mother, compared to around five per cent of couple-mothers. As such, 70 per cent of lone mothers received means-tested allowances or transfers of some sort, like housing assistance, compared with 22 per cent of couple households. While means testing in Sweden has been comparatively limited compared to the UK, the proportion of lone mothers receiving a housing allowance was 81 per cent in 1993, compared to 20 per cent of couples with children. High participation in the housing benefit system means that a lone mother considering increasing her labour supply faces reduced housing benefits, with composite marginal tax rates reaching 90 per cent.

As elsewhere, lone mothers, along with immigrants, are far more likely to be long-term welfare recipients. During the period 1983-1992, nearly 14 per cent of lone mothers received social assistance for three out of ten years, compared to just over five per cent of couple-mothers. The picture was worse for lone fathers, at 19 per cent.[59] All in all:

> ...data... indicate that the 'feminisation of poverty' is now emerging as a phenomenon in Sweden as it has in many other countries. Low-paid jobs are a part of this picture, as is the increased precariousness of lone mothers' attachment to the labour market and discrimination against them—particularly when they have small children.[60]

The growth of welfare dependency is part of a pattern of growing drop-out from the labour market and increasing housing segregation, where the dream towns of the urban planners have become, as elsewhere, sinks of disadvantage. The pattern was spreading in the 1980s, a time of high overall employment and economic growth, and was decisively reinforced by the recession of the early 1990s. Between 1988 and 1997, employment among young people aged 16-34 fell off by about 400,000; only a minority of this was due to educational expansion. In 'disadvantaged' districts, or areas where low-income earners are at least ten times as numerous as high-income earners, nearly one-third of all households with children in 1990 were lone-parent families, compared with one-tenth in areas of high income. In some districts, nearly half of the children and young people were recipients of social allowance.

Given the persistence, and even growth, of problems, despite the assumption that all family forms are equal, or made so by progressive policies: 'The national discourse on lone mothers in Sweden could be interpreted as moving from an emphasis on lone mothers as part of a lifestyle change, towards lone mothers as a social problem. Lone mothers are increasingly portrayed as one of the groups that have fared less well than others during the restructuring of the economy in Sweden since the 1980s.'[61]

By the 1980s, claimants for social assistance also included a high proportion of single, young and often childless people, a situation now emerging in the UK. Sweden has one of the biggest unemployment gaps between the majority population and non-European immigrants of all industrialised nations. At seven per cent, the poverty rate among non-elderly households without children was higher in Sweden than in the UK. The reasons lie in alcohol/drug abuse, and mental or physical illness, plus refugees from outside the Nordic area and assorted drop-outs who do not fulfil the criteria for mainstream benefits and who cannot, or do not want to, work. Single men without children make up about a third of Sweden's welfare caseload.

There has been some reduction in welfare dependency since the late 1990s, and in 2001 a target for 'social justice' was set substantially to reduce the numbers whose income is lower than basic subsistence, halve the sick leave rate by 2008, and cut dependence on social assistance by a half by 2004—an ambitious programme involving a reduction on the level of 1990.[62]

Divorce is disadvantageous—even in Sweden

Divorce still disadvantages Swedish women. They earn less than men, and, given economies of scale, the division of the household into two implies than an increase in total income is necessary to maintain former living standards. If there had been no welfare benefits or other programmes, the income of divorced women would have been only two-thirds that of individuals in intact families in 1990. After divorce, men contribute less to supporting their children and former spouse.[63] The situation of Swedish women without children is even worse after divorce than it is for mothers since they do not qualify for the income transfers.

As much as lone parenthood is still disadvantageous in Sweden, so marriage remains advantageous. In all countries, from Japan to the USA, married couples see income and wealth grow over time, compared to lone adult families and households. Analysis of the *Swedish Level of Living Survey*, from 1981 to 1991, showed how divorced women with children had significantly poorer income growth than intact couples. Couples improved their adjusted median income by 24 per cent whereas the lone mothers increased theirs by four per cent. All the fiscal manipulation cannot compensate for the ways that value is added and well-being increased within families by co-operation, a division of labour, specialisation and economies of scale. Dividing up households will always have a negative effect on living standards,[64] even when governments strip marriage of all fiscal support. Larger households have higher living standards. This benefits everyone, as can be seen with international comparisons. In Southern Europe, the situation of young people is favourable compared to age-peers in the North, since they share in the parents' living standards by remaining in the parental home until relatively late in life. Elderly people on small incomes also have a higher material standard since they are more likely to share with adult children.

Insofar as couples pool their resources, a divorce or separation by necessity implies a decline in economic circumstances, particularly for the partner who contributes the smaller share of income. Moreover, a divorce will affect the economic circumstances of both parties due to a loss of economies of scale and social capital. Even in Sweden, lone parents have more problems reconciling work with family responsibilities (34 per cent compared to 25 per cent of married mothers), presumably because, despite all the childcare, they have no help at home.[65] While much is made of the importance of paternal leave from work to care for children where there are couples, the implications of the loss of help at home for lone parents appears to be completely ignored. And, while Sweden is supposed to be a model of co-operative parenting, whether or not the parents are married, more than 50 per cent of lone mothers complain that the fathers take little responsibility for their children.[66]

In recent cohorts, the socio-economic and educational differences between married and divorced households owe much to downward mobility. Disruption is associated with declining housing standards as well as income loss. Most lone mothers rent their homes, while 80 per cent of 'partnered' women own theirs. Downward mobility effects are also an explanation for the socio-economic differences between households with an unmarried couple and those where two previously cohabiting adults have separated. High numbers of people living alone also mean high levels of low-income households, or over 30 per cent of working-age, one-person households in 2001.[67]

Men as well?

For men, the negative effects on income from the loss of the partner are cancelled out by the positive effects of not living with children and having responsibility for them. However, income growth for a large minority of divorced men is relatively poor. In one large-scale study, half of the divorced men had a rise in income comparable to that of other men, but a quarter had a real factor income in 1990 that was two-thirds or less of what it had been ten years before. Some men had income drops from high levels, but others worked less or not at all; most of these were under 55. This points to the same loss or absence of the work ethic seen for single, separated and divorced men elsewhere.

Everywhere, male cohabitants with children have rates of economic inactivity and attainment that resemble those of single and divorced men and, again, Sweden is no exception. Analysis based on data collected by the *Swedish Commission on Educational Inequality*[68] shows non-married two-parent households to have markedly lower occupational and educational attainment compared to married parents. This is only partly because cohabiting couples are, on average, younger than married parents.

Less well-being

The 1990s saw a marked deterioration in mental health for all age groups before retirement, with almost twice as many women sufferers as men. Young people, especially young women, saw the biggest decline. Sick leave rates have generally increased for all illness, but the increase is most marked for mental illness. There is a fourfold higher risk of divorced men acquiring a psychiatric record, compared to comparable married men and two-and-a-half times the risk for divorced women.[69] On every mental health indicator, lone mothers report negatives more frequently than couple- or married mothers, and make more suicide attempts.[70] As many as a quarter of Swedish lone mothers say that they have feelings of inadequacy and are often tired. This is surprising, considering that the lone mother sample was skewed towards younger mothers, compared to the married sample.[71]

There is little evidence that divorcees are selected out of marriage by having a permanently lower psychological well-being, or that this accounts for more than a small amount of the increased risk.[72] In turn, decreased well-being was only partly explained by economic circumstances, time allocation, frequency of contact with friends or relatives and access to social support; something seen in other studies.[73] Research from elsewhere suggests that the adverse psychological effects increase over time more for men than for women following a divorce.[74]

The physical health of lone mothers is poor in Sweden as well as in Britain, and the size of the gap with couple- mothers is similar in both countries (using a comparative analysis of 17 years of the *British General Household Survey* and the *Swedish Survey of Living Conditions*).[75] For lone mothers, poor health runs at nearly double the rate for couple-mothers, and rates of limiting long-standing illness are between 50 per cent and 60 per cent higher.[76] The prevalence of less than good health increases over time among poor lone mothers, while rates decline slightly for poor couple-mothers, widening the health gap between the two, and suggesting factors buffering the effects for poor couple-mothers. Among lone and couple-mothers who were not poor, there was no change. Lone mothers who were not poor had a significantly higher rate of limiting long-standing illness than non-poor couple-mothers. Poor health was also significantly higher among employed lone mothers than among employed couple-mothers, with prevalence among lone mothers increasing over time.

Differentials in mortality as well as in health for married and unmarried people are observed in Sweden as elsewhere, despite all the attempts to engineer equal outcomes. Single Swedish men and women are at a higher risk of dying, largely due to heart and circulatory disease, than the married.[77] Whilst smoking and alcohol abuse are more prevalent amongst divorced men, even non-smoking and non-alcoholic divorced men still have twice the mortality rate of married men.[78] On the assumption that the poor socioeconomic status of lone mothers contributes to higher mortality, as well as health selection factors, one study analysed the mortality of 90,111 lone mothers compared to 622,365 'partnered' women.[79] The differences were only reduced by the controls, and increased with the length of lone parenthood. In particular, couple-women had the smallest risk of dying from suicide, assault, homicide, or alcohol-related causes, while mothers without a 'partner' had almost a four-fold risk of committing suicide and a five-fold risk of being a victim of violence or dying from alcohol-related causes. Cases of assaults on women have risen with a general rise in violent crime. Lone mothers are the most vulnerable to threats and violence, particularly where they have other welfare and health-related problems.[80]

Since Swedish policies support parents who work, and work full-time, it is claimed that any 'additional social and economic pressures lone mothers may have because they are the sole breadwinner and carer for the family, can become hidden or made invisible'.[81] Contrary to the continual reiteration in the UK of the mantra that lone parents problems will be solved if they all went to work, observers of the Swedish situation suggest that lone mothers should be given the chance to work less—which must imply more welfare dependency.

Children of lone parents in Sweden

Since there are a sufficiently large number of one-parent families to provide reliable comparisons on outcomes, studies of the life-chances for children in one-parent and two-parent families are relatively easy in Sweden. They can help answer the question as to whether goals of equal life-chances for children in one-parent and two-parent families have resulted in equal outcomes. It is confidently asserted that 'Swedish evidence suggests that if there is any difference between the children of lone mothers and those in couple-families with the same social and economic circumstances, it is that the former are more mature and self sufficient'.[82]

So Swedish lone-parent children have *superior* outcomes? Assessments of overall and all-cause mortality between 1991 and 1998 of a million Swedish children showed that those of lone parents had a higher risk of death than those with two parents, which was most pronounced for those aged 13-17.[83] The risk was more than 50 per cent greater for boys with lone parents than for boys with two parents. Boys of lone parents were more than five times more likely to die from drug or alcohol abuse, more than three times as likely to die from a fall or poisoning, and more than four times as likely to die from violence. While the overall death rate for girls of lone parents did not differ much from that of girls with two parents, girls with one parent were more than twice as likely to commit suicide, and more than three times as likely to die from drugs or alcohol abuse, than girls with two parents. Furthermore, contrary to myths spread by child-protection lobbyists in the UK, Sweden does not have Europe's lowest number of deaths from child abuse as a result of being the first country in the world to ban smacking. Figures from Unicef show that deaths from child maltreatment during a five-year period in the 1990s occurred at an annual rate of 0.5 or 0.6 children per 100,000 aged under 15 in Sweden, compared with 0.4 or 0.9 in the UK, depending on whether or not unconfirmed cases were included.[84] The countries with the lowest child maltreatment death rates are mainly Catholic and traditional countries like Greece, Italy, Spain and Ireland, that have had low rates of both lone parenthood and government supervision of families. Smacking has not been criminalised in any of these countries.[85] Sweden saw a 489 per cent increase in physical child abuse

49

cases classified as criminal assaults from 1981-1994, and a fivefold increase in child-on-child criminal assaults between 1984 and 1994.[86]

Mediators (intermediate paths through which lone parenthood might affect children's health and well-being, like welfare receipt, renting or owning a house, number of children), and confounders (factors which might independently affect outcomes, like the age of parents and children, country of birth, place of residence, socioeconomic status, psychiatric disease and addiction of parents), reduced the connections by less than half. It seems that family structure has about the same importance as socio-economic affiliation as a predictor.

As well as increased mortality, children of lone parents also had more than double the risk of psychiatric disorder, suicide attempts and injury, and more than three times the risk of addictions.[87] Just as they had higher risks than girls from all-cause mortality, boys with lone parents also had higher risks than girls for psychiatric disease and drug-related problems.

According to the Swedish Commission on Educational Inequality (which studied 120,000 students between 1988 and 1992), children who had been through family dissolution showed lower educational attainment at 16 than those in stable two-parent families. The children of lone parents did better than those living with two unmarried adults, and the children of widow(er)s better than those of divorced parents.[88] Indeed, children's attainment is markedly lower in reconstituted families consisting of non-married adults than in lone-parent families. It seems that children of divorced parents, or those with reconstituted families and those whose parents are cohabiting, are less likely to continue schooling after the compulsory level, and even if they do, are less likely to continue to the upper secondary level than are children whose parents are married. Children whose parents are married are more likely to choose an upper secondary education than are other children, so this is attained by 38 per cent of children of married parents born into the unskilled manual working class, but only 31 per cent of those with single parents. All this is likely to impact on socio-economic circumstances in later life.

As elsewhere, leaving school early predisposes youngsters to form early 'partnerships' and early parenthood. In turn, these are associated with an increased risk of later separation or divorce, as part of intergenerational patterns of family fragmentation.[89] Women who experience the separation of their parents are more likely to cohabit than those who have not—even given Sweden's high rate of cohabitation. The proportion of women aged 20-39 who have ever cohabited is 61 per cent for those whose parents had divorced, compared to 50 per cent for those whose parents remained married.[90] In turn, Swedish women who leave home early have—throughout childhood and adolescence—more strained family relations, poorer adjustment, higher rates of school problems, lower educational aspirations, more drinking and drug taking, earlier sexual activity, and more sexual partners, than their peers who leave home later. It is not so much that early home-leaving disrupts educational plans, but that low educational aspirations are part of a pattern set in motion long before leaving home.[91] The greater tendency to leave school early for children of lone-parent, cohabiting and 'reconstituted' families is related to poorer performance in school as well as to educational decisions at given levels of performance.

Income explains very little of these family type variations in Sweden, where income differences and dispersion are anyway smaller than in, for example, the US. Cohabiting parents and reconstituted families are also characterised by lower social and educational attainment, even if their disposable income per household unit is similar to that of married couples. Downward social mobility, through losing the parent with the highest education and class position, explains more of the differences for lone-parent children. When educational and occupational attainment is low for custodial mothers but high for absent fathers, children are most negatively affected by a separation. However, after controlling for these conditions and also housing characteristics and number of siblings, there still remains a statistically significant difference between children with married parents and those in other family types. Especially for early school-leaving, there is a substantial net effect of family dissolution. It replicates the results of an investigation of early home-leaving in America (based on the 1988 *National Survey of Families and Households*), which showed how children in non-intact families seek early independence and are less likely to attend higher education, irrespective of the parents' economic status.[92]

Longitudinal studies also indicate that staying with a continuously lone parent is more beneficial to the child's schooling than the parent's remarriage, given the lower attainment in step- compared to lone-parent families. Conversely, the departure of a step-parent has a positive effect on educational attainment. A new adult may not only mean more disruption, but the quality of parenting may be lower in step-families compared to families with two biological parents, or even one parent. Children involved in family reconstitution may have to take second place to children born to their own parent and step-parent or be displaced by their step-parents' own children.[93] In UK and US cohort research, many step-parents show little or no interest in children's progress, want the children to leave school at the earliest possible opportunity, and have the lowest aspirations for employment. Moreover, 're-partnered' mothers may be comparatively uninterested in their children, especially where they have sons, being less involved and sharing fewer activities, with their time and allegiance monopolised by the new husband or boyfriend.[94] This difference in investment probably explains the way that offspring of mothers who remarried had lower educational achievement (by over one year) than those whose mothers did not remarry in the *US Study of Marital Instability over the Life Course.*[95]

Long-term effects

Indications are that Swedish individuals who experience family disruption, hardship or dissension in childhood have poorer outcomes in terms of illness and mortality. Those whose family backgrounds were characterised by severe conflict go on to have the lowest well-being as adults in terms of mortality and mental and physical illness. After controlling for the effect of socio-economic and other variables and other types of child-hood problems, their relative mortality was 52 per cent higher.[96]

These results for Sweden are consistent with research on other western countries. For example, in one US study parental divorce took an average of four years off the life expectancy of adult children whose parents divorced before they were 21.[97] A longitudinal study that tracked a white, middle-class, high IQ sample, found a significantly higher mortality rate among those whose parents divorced. Forty-year-olds from divorced homes were three times as likely to die from all causes as 40-year-olds whose parents had stayed married.[98] Another study found that the mortality difference was enhanced when the divorce took place before the child's fourth birthday.[99]

Intergenerational effects are not only present in the propensity for women who experienced the separation of their parents to have more casual and disrupted relationships in later life, but greater dependency on means-related benefits. The 1992/3 *Swedish Family Survey* showed that 30 per cent of women who grew up with a lone parent received social assistance at least once during the period 1983-1992, compared with 15 per cent of women who grew up with two parents.[100] Rates are even higher for men who grew up with a lone parent at nearly 40 per cent. Unemployment benefit receipt shows a similar, but smaller, differentiation by family background. This is not explainable in terms of earning capacity. The finances of those growing up with lone parents are, like their private lives, more fragmented.

Equality for women?

Sweden's pro-natalist policies have always been presented in a 'gender equality' gift-wrapping. So it is appropriate to assess the success of these policies by their impact on women's position in society and the labour force.

As the proportion of working women with school-age children rose, an estimated 85 per cent of mothers of under-sevens were in the workforce by 1984. Sweden had become the leader of the Western world for women's work outside the home. Or had it? What Sweden had was a high percentage of women working part-time or only nominally in the workforce. By 1981, 46 per cent of women employees worked part-time. Whereas earlier it was chiefly older women who worked part-time, most of the increase under the equality programme was among women aged 25-35. The average number of hours worked by all women actually dropped. This was accounted for by mothers taking on part-time work after the birth of a child, instead of giving up work as they used to, and then remaining in part-time work when a second child was born.

Their jobs were often poorly paid and irregular. The increase over time of Swedish women in better paid and higher status employment, as elsewhere in the twentieth century, was largely a function of the absence of dependent children, either throughout, or at both ends of the working life. It is misconceived to imagine that childcare, or the transfer of domestic tasks to the market, or collective sector, could ever put mothers on an equal footing with childless women or men.

Until parental leave enabled women to stay at home for long periods, another unintended effect was the increase in the number of women who relinquished motherhood entirely. As in the old Soviet societies, the necessity for two wage-earners simply pushed down family size. A half of Swedish families had one child; the average woman had only 1.63 children in 1983, and about 25 per cent of pregnancies were aborted. Yet, a family of two was favoured by a majority of women of all ages, with one child preferred by only ten per cent, and 25 per cent desiring three or more children.[101] It would seem that women made the best compromise they could between the minimum amount of paid employment consonant with maintaining a reasonable living standard, and the number of children they could care for while balancing a job with running a home. This both restricted mothers' job opportunities while they had young children, and their ultimate family size.

Sweden has a more gender-segregated workforce than the USA, the UK and Germany. Indeed, it is more gender-segregated than Asian countries like China, Hong Kong and

India. Only the Islamic Middle East and Africa, and certain developing countries, have similar or higher levels of occupational segregation.[102] The expansion of welfare occupations has resulted in women being increasingly concentrated in clerical and welfare work. By 1985, women accounted for 87 per cent of total health/education/ welfare employment. Women in Sweden have not been employed as substitutes for male workers in industry and commerce, but have been the beneficiaries of the expansion of welfare services from the 1960s. Out went unpaid domestic work and in came the state as provider *and* employer. Sex equality legislation, positive discrimination and trade union pressure may have improved women's wages and salaries compared with men's, but this has had little effect on vertical and horizontal segregation. The high social costs, absenteeism and disruptions to production that are connected with women's employment lead private employers to prefer men. Swedish experience demonstrates how 'policies that push all women into employment, irrespective of preferences, are incompatible with sex equality in the workforce'.[103] Social scientists are slowly beginning to admit that Swedish pro-natalist 'gender equality' policies necessarily produce high levels of sex segregation in the labour market and a large pay gap.[104] Even *Swedish* social scientists are beginning to admit that family-friendly social policies are incompatible with policies to achieve gender equality in the labour market, and that Sweden has a larger glass-ceiling problem than the USA, where family-friendly policies are almost non-existent.[105]

The decline in the family as an economic unit has meant that the extended public sector has taken over many of the tasks that were previously carried out unpaid by women in the home, such as care of children and the elderly. As this opened up 'gainful' employment for more women, the same expansion of the public sector also increased the demand for labour. Not least, the expansion of public childcare has created jobs for a large number of (mainly female) child-minders and pre-school teachers. Sustained full employment, especially women's full employment, has had to rely on public sector jobs in Scandinavia, with manufacturing employment in decline. Until the mid-1980s, when its expansion came to a halt, this sector accounted for roughly 80 per cent of job growth in Denmark and Sweden. While there are small wage differences between men and women in the same occupation and industry, after controlling for education, experience, etc., men still earned more than women in the 1990s. Most important, men still earned two-thirds to three-quarters of family income. The overall pay gap in Sweden (and all Nordic countries) is much the same as in other societies.[106] The work histories and work patterns of men and women in Sweden differ qualitatively, even if women spend more time in market work than those in some other European countries. Men tend to dominate in positions of responsibility and authority, especially in the private sector which, unlike the public sector, is not so bound by positive discrimination.

Catherine Hakim condemns as a 'practical impossibility' the notion that 'egalitarian and family-friendly policies can eliminate the conflict between two such different, time-consuming, and demanding activities' as family and career, 'so that people who do take time out for family work are "not disadvantaged" in their careers compared with those who do not take time out for a family break'.[107]

For most women, their jobs are not so central to them as they are for men, and they do not have a one-track life. In turn, the alternative of economic dependence with a focus on family work hardly appeals to more than a small minority of men. Most women are secondary earners whose needs and interests differ from those of primary earners.

If sexual differentiation in the labour market persists after Sweden's years of commitment to egalitarian policies, what chance of equal outcomes elsewhere?

The Potemkin workforce

Much of Swedish employment has been paper employment, with very high absenteeism. The extent of paid leave for sickness, holidays, parenting, etc., means that women take two to three times as much paid time off than men. Such 'paid absenteeism' means that, on any given day, 20 per cent of female workers are off on some kind of paid leave, or 30 per cent in the public sector. For mothers of children under three, the proportion was 48 per cent, four times the national average for all workers in 1990. A 'very large share of what is normally regarded as labour time is in fact "welfare time"'.[108] The levels of sickness amongst both men and women are far higher than in other countries, reflecting generous sick pay schemes. In 1990, employers became responsible for the first two weeks of sickness to cut down abuse of the scheme.

Not that it was the employers' fault. Indeed, in the spring of 1980, Goteborg's Volvo plant decided to solve the problem of high labour costs, absenteeism, and 'blue-collar blues' not by redesigning jobs (as Volvo did in the 1970s), but rather by becoming the European leader in the introduction of industrial robots.[109]

It did not do much good. By 2005, the rate of sick leave had again almost doubled since the late 1990s. On an average day, nearly a fifth of Sweden's potential workforce was either off sick or on disability benefits. Surging absenteeism provoked sterner calls from international bodies like the Organisation for Economic Co-operation and Development and the International Monetary Fund to do something to improve the labour market by reining in out-of-work benefits, parental leave and payments for study and sabbatical leaves, as well as improving conditions for small businesses faced with tax rates twice as high as the EU average.[110]

Super kids?

High levels of sickness may also be a consequence of daycare. In the former East Germany and other socialist countries, children had higher sickness rates due to contagion in state nurseries. Mothers have to take time off work to care for them at home, or because they themselves have been infected by their child. It was calculated that, in Hungary, mothers with young children spent up to 50 per cent of their annual work time at home on maternity or sick-leave (30-40 per cent on child sick-leave alone). The cost of homecare allowances for mothers proved to be one-third of the cost of providing 'socialised' childcare.[111]

In the 1980s in Sweden, daycare for children under 18 months was effectively abandoned and considerably run down for the under-threes (with some municipalities offering no nursery places for children in this age group), due to the immense costs of looking after babies properly, and reports of adverse outcomes. Paying mothers to care for their children at home on 'leave' also maintains the fiction that these women are in continuous employment. In some accounts, the babies of mothers on parental leave are included in public care statistics.

It is not sufficiently appreciated by those who eulogise about Swedish childcare that there are few places available for very young children. In general, standards have been high in Swedish childcare, compared to the situation in the US and UK. Child nurses have two years of special training and pre-school teachers an extra two-and-a-half years of training after leaving college. There have usually been 12 children in the younger age groups (up to two-and-a-half-years) and 15-16 in the older groups of three- to seven-year-olds, and with four staff. Where problems have been suggested, there has been a tactical retreat. Since Sweden generally provides closely controlled care of a similar quality, this may have diminished its impact on child development, so that it generally has very little or no effect over and above that of the child's social class and family background.[112] Moreover, Sweden has not produced super children as a result of day care. As elsewhere, there are suggestions that it is only children of less educated parents who show any benefit from day care and that children of highly educated parents are more competent when they stay at home in the early years.

The big rise in the birth rate in the late 1980s was used to illustrate the benefits of putting mothers into the workforce,[113] when it owes more to their opportunities to withdraw from it and look after their own children at home. This pattern is familiar: births rise as male incomes or women's unearned income rises. The reduction in the mother's opportunity costs from paid leave raises the value of her time at home, instead of this appearing 'wasteful', and also increases the status of having children. With role conflict reduced to manageable levels, the birth rate ascends.

Reducing full-time hours to part-time hours, or six hours a day for parents, also helps keep record numbers of employees working full-time, even if it is a ghost labour force. Swedish accounts of their triumphant system are reminiscent of Soviet propaganda, with the low birth rates of the 1960s and 1970s attributed to the way that women felt like 'pioneers in the labour market'.[114]

The 'collective house', or the domestic equivalent of the day nursery, was an unmitigated failure—apart from a few radicals, people simply did not want to live in them. Tried from the 1930s onwards, they floundered on high costs and low demand, and the last ones shut down in the late 1970s.

An end of gender?

Do women put their jobs first, as planned? Not really. Swedish women generally consider that any lack of balance between work and family works to the detriment of the family, not the job. Earning money is given as the most important reason for work by 70 per cent of women.[115] The majority of parents do not use parental leave to finance part-time work, but to take a complete break. Married mothers with pre-school children tend to have higher rates of short part-time work, but long part-time (20-24 hours per week) is more prevalent among married than lone mothers. This is often the minimum time that day nurseries will take children.

Household work is strongly divided by gender. Women continue to perform the larger part of unpaid household duties. This is decried by state functionaries, although when both paid and unpaid work are taken into consideration, men and women work roughly the same number of hours (as is also the case in Britain).

Despite the widely publicised 'working parties' to study and engineer men's role change, and the ways in which changes in family law are explicitly designed to force couples to share breadwinning, housework and childcare, men's parental leave-taking has been minimal—unless compelled. Sharing leave is inconvenient, since both parties have to keep leaving and returning to the workforce. Surveys of new parents showed that most Swedish mothers did not want to share the care of babies with the father.[116] Leave-taking is often interpreted by employers and colleagues as signifying low commitment to the job. Couples feel more secure developing one principal occupation (even if, alone, it does not provide enough to live on), than having two insubstantial jobs. The higher the father's income, the less leave he takes, while men with women who earn more, both absolutely and relatively, are less likely to take leave.[117] Investigations to find out which factors had the strongest independent effects on preferences reveal the overwhelming importance of attitudes. Three-quarters of fathers and two-thirds of mothers still believed in the 1980s than men should be the principal breadwinners, and almost equally they believe that success at work is more important for men.

This is despite continual exposure to 'unconventional' role models, educational efforts to 'restructure sex models', aptitudes and preferences, and the removal of any suggestions of conventional male or female concerns. As in China, moral exhortation has been a primary tool of social engineering in Sweden.[118] However the change in the tax law is regarded as the reform that has done the most to 'promote equality between the sexes' by changing behaviour, if not attitudes.[119] Women went to work because they had to, were forced to, and would not have done so had they had any choice. However, the touching faith in the ability to re-design people has had tremendous tenacity. One commentator tells us to:

> ...imagine that if an equal division of the parental leave were to be written into the parental insurance law as a condition of eligibility, it could lead to a society of men whose energies were divided between their jobs and their children, and of women who identified with their work outside the home instead of

concentrating on keeping their men in shape and preparing their children for the workforce.[120]

One view blames the successful incorporation of social feminism into mainstream politics for holding back the development of a more critical (read Marxist) and radical (read lesbian separatist) feminist movement. Because policy was never radical enough, complete androgyny, with all children in daycare and women in equal numbers with men in all occupations, at all times of life, has not been achieved. This is not to do with the fact that women may not want it, but because they were 'devoured by equality under the terms of a male value system...'[121] Because everything was done to ensure equal outcomes, women were oppressed. The Scandinavian state is just a 'tutelary state' for women. Women remain in a secondary capacity, because men have craftily consolidated their power by taking all the senior positions in the public sector as well as dominating the private sector.

Inequalities

The income differences between generations are large, and have increased substantially in the last 20 years. The increase in poverty in the 1990s affected families with children, especially those with lone parents, numerous children, and families with young children. Couples without children, especially at older ages, were unaffected. The living conditions and incomes of 20-29-year-olds have generally declined. Among men and women aged 20-29, poverty increased sharply during the 1990s, but remained consistently low for the over-45s. This is related to longer education periods, growing youth unemployment, and earnings which begin later in life and are more insecure. Pensioners have experienced the most favourable develop-ments in incomes, and have not been affected by the economic crisis of the 1990s, experiencing an increase of 10-13 per cent in their disposable income, while lone parents saw a fall of six per cent and couples with children saw a fall of four per cent.

From the mid-1980s, the generational differences between young adults and the elderly increased to become as large as the corresponding class differences.[122] Generational differences are greater in the Nordic countries than in the EU as a whole. As elsewhere, unemployment since the 1970s has been predominantly a youth problem. In Southern Europe, it is quite common to remain in the parental home even to age 30 and beyond, and thereby get the economies of scale that a large household offers. In terms of the percentage of the parents' material standards, the situation of young Swedish people is less favourable than that of age-mates in Southern European countries. In spite of later entry to the labour market, the move from the parental home is only marginally delayed.

4. Why is Sweden Held Up as the Model?

In 1982, it appeared that Sweden was 'moving faster than most other advanced industrialised countries toward a society of cohabiting individuals, temporary families, and single individuals with and without children'.[123] Even now, when we can see how this Utopia of state direction and beneficence is itself beginning to crack, many European countries still look to Sweden as the model for social and family policy, despite the fragmented society it creates.

Those who hold up Sweden as the model for family policy in the UK fail to recognise that its centralised decision-making systems may be too rigid and unwieldy to cope with the changing, complex and diversifying conditions of modern economies, where there is far more global, unrestricted (or unrestrictable) information exchange.[124] There is also a European trend away from the funding of day care and towards cash allowances for parents of young children to use for their own or alternative care and which are not tied to any particular work patterns or requirements, as in Finland and Norway. Austrian interest in such schemes prompted research by the Austrian Institute of Family Studies[125] which showed that only around one per cent of women wanted men to stay home looking after children. Not many more wanted to share parental leave with men, or to return to work shortly after giving birth (significantly, only childless people agreed to any marked extent). The most popular options, as elsewhere, were for women to stay at home until children reached their school years, or for at least two years. There is an inexorable logic about all of this. Falling birth rates and the cost and unpopularity of childcare in the former Sovietised Eastern bloc countries also prompted moves towards family allowances and tax relief rather than crèches. The Swedish model is looking a somewhat tired one to emulate.

3

Italy: Hotel Mama is Closing Down

1. The Present Situation

The main characteristics of family formation in Italy in recent decades are:

- the traditional family, based on marriage, with support across generations, is more intact in Italy than elsewhere;
- Italy has exceptionally low fertility: the birth rate had fallen to 1.18 by 1995, with completed fertility estimated at 1.47 children per woman, and only recovered to 1.26 in 2002.
- an ageing population. In 1996 Italy became the first country in the world where old people outnumber young people;
- births outside marriage remain among the lowest in Europe;
- delayed marriage is increasingly common;
- cohabitation remains low enough to be almost invisible, even among the young;
- separation and divorce are increasing, but remain among the lowest in Europe;
- migration has replaced natural population growth as the main source of population increase.

Home of the traditional family

While 28.4 per cent of households in the UK in the mid-1990s contained a married couple and children, in Italy this was 39.6 per cent—beaten only by Ireland, Portugal and Spain. Only 0.1 per cent were a cohabiting couple with children, compared with two per cent in the UK. Similarly, around 0.1 per cent of households were cohabitees without children, compared with nearly four per cent in the UK. In turn, while 20.5 per cent of Italian households were married without children, this was over 23 per cent in the UK. There are more complex households in Italy: nearly ten per cent compared with six per cent of all households in Britain. Household size is higher than in the UK. Households of four or more persons made up 35 per cent or more of Italian households versus 22 per cent in the UK.

Almost all children (90 per cent) under 18 live with both their parents. Around eight per cent live with one parent, compared with 22 per cent in the UK. Children stay at home longer in Italy. About 90 per cent of those under 24 live at home with parents, even if they have a job. Staying in Hotel Mama is increasingly popular: 33 per cent of those aged 25-34 stayed at home in 1993, up from 22 per cent in 1983.

Births — and the lack of them

The fertility rate is about 40 per cent lower than the replacement threshold that would ensure population replacement or stability. By 2000, the fertility rate per Italian woman was 1.18, although rising to 1.26 in 2002. Completed fertility is estimated at 1.47 in 2000. The age of women at first birth has been high since the 1970s, and rose to nearly 30 years in the mid-1990s. In 1996, Italy became the first country in the world where old people outnumber young people. Only 14 per cent of the population are 15 and under, while nearly 18 per cent (in 2000) are 65 and over. Together with Ireland, it is showing the greatest decrease in the proportion of the young (under 20) and in the working-age group (20-59). By the year 2050 the percentage difference between the population aged 0 to 19 and 60 and over, and those of working age 20-60, will be the highest in Europe after Spain. Dependency levels will be such that there will be close to 140 young and elderly people to every 100 of working age.[1]

The natural population increase is now negative: -0.4 per 1,000 inhabitants. The population increases, however, by 2.8 per 1,000 people due to migration. Net migration is 3.1 per 1,000 people. Thus, Italy's net migration rate is the highest in the EU, even beating Spain and the UK—the other countries with very high net migration rates. Immigration is the *de facto* substitute for fertility, accounting for 80 per cent of the population growth in the EU.

Infant and under-fives mortality rates have fallen sharply, by at least 50 per cent in Italy, Portugal and Spain over the years 1980 to 1994, but are still high compared with Northern European countries. Infant mortality in Italy was 8.6 for the mid-1990s, compared with 6.6 for the UK and 5.8 for Sweden. Under-fives mortality was 8.0 compared with 7.0 and 5.0.

In Italy, extra-marital births were around eight per cent in 1995 (versus 34 per cent in Britain), and 9.7 per cent in 2000 (40 per cent in the UK). This compares with 2.2 per cent in 1970 (eight per cent in the UK). Teenage births are very low in Italy (nine per 1,000 women aged 15-19), and the lowest in the West after the Netherlands (at seven).

Marriage

Italians marry late. Over 60 per cent of Italian women aged 20-29 were single in 1996. Given a low divorce rate by European standards, the percentage of marriages which are first marriages for Italian women was still 96 per cent in the mid-1990s (compared with nearly 72 per cent in Britain). The mean age at first marriage is 30 for men and 27 for women—much as in the UK (30 for men and 28 for women).

Cohabitation

While over a third of women aged 20-29 were cohabiting in Sweden in 1996, and just over 12 per cent in Britain, cohabitation remains under three per cent in all southern and Catholic countries, including Greece, Ireland, Spain and Portugal, as well as Italy.

Italy has the lowest levels of repeat partnerships, with one per cent or less among women aged 35-39 having three or more 'partnerships'.[2] For a majority of women in Italy and Spain, marriage still means the start of the first live-in relationship.

More single cohabiting mothers marry than in Britain. France and Britain have the lowest proportion of single, cohabiting mothers who marry at around one-third. It is higher in Sweden, where 56 per cent marry within five years, and highest in Italy, with 70 per cent marrying.[3]

Divorce

Italy's low divorce levels set it apart from many other European countries. However, from 1971 to 2000, separations (which must proceed divorce) have grown by nearly 170 per cent, and divorces by 60 per cent. (About 140 combined per 100,000 inhabitants, or 0.7 per 1,000, compared with the British rate of 2.7 divorces per 1,000 people and 2.25 in Sweden.) The number of 'reconstituted' couples was calculated for the first time in Italy in 1993/4 at 4.2 per cent of all couples. In 40 per cent of these there are no children. Two-thirds are remarried.

Comparisons with north-west Europe

The change in the never-married population in many north and western European countries has a lot to do with the replacement of marriage with cohabitation. Spain and Italy show a marked decline in any 'partnerships', with the lowest rates of cohabitation in Europe, while Sweden has the highest. Thirty-five per cent of men aged 30-34 have never 'partnered' (76 for those aged 25-29). For women it is 17 and 47 respectively.

The same intergenerational effects of family disintegration are present in Italy. Women who have experienced the separation of their parents are more likely to cohabit than those who have not—even if there is less cohabitation anyway. The percentage of women aged 20-39 who had ever cohabited was 15 per cent for those whose parents had divorced, compared with three per cent for those whose parents remained married, while 67 and 89 per cent respectively married directly.[4]

2. The Historical Background

The Italian family remains typical of what may be classified as the Mediterranean model. There is a high level of stability, low fertility, low levels of cohabitation, late and falling marriage and few births out of wedlock. Few women are in the labour market, and many young people stay in the family home into their 20s and 30s, as noted in Tables 1 and 2 (pp. 7-10).

Because of the strong family-centred cultural traditions, Southern European countries have poorly developed public family policies. Historically, there has not been the diversity or longevity of horizontal equity measures seen in other advanced countries. Such measures came mainly to Italy during the Fascist period. In the 1930s, the most important were explicitly designed to raise the birth rate, and involved marriage loans, wedding and birth bonuses, tax reductions and family allowances according to the number of children or other family dependents, and a 'bachelor tax' on single men. Women were seen as being at the service of the family, and for rearing future soldiers. A decree of 1938 limited the employment of women in public and private offices, and forbade companies with fewer than ten employees to take on female personnel. Maternal and infant welfare measures were strongly developed in the UK on a charitable, self-help, municipal and then state level—not least to tackle high infant mortality—by the late nineteenth century. In Italy, this was muted and similar measures awaited the establishment of the National Institute for Maternity and Infancy (OMNI) in the 1930s (abolished in 1975 as local authorities took over social services).

The development of measures to support the family, let alone any aspiration to raise marriage or birth rates, is often represented as reactionary and repressive, if not racist. This association is particularly strong in Italy. The heavy-handed interference of the state in the family sphere under fascism provoked a strong reaction. This contributes to the distinctiveness of Italian family policy, where the family meets the burden of primary social needs with little assistance but, also, without much interference. Social and family policies have been minimal or residual, at the same time as individuals have really nowhere else to meet their needs other than in the family or the marketplace. Social welfare is only meant to complement the resources provided in the first instance by the family. On the whole, there has been indifference or hostility to any proposed measures to raise the astonishingly low birth rate, whether direct or indirect, and however they might facilitate the family choices desired by women. This has not been allied, as in Anglophone countries, to a sour or critical stance on the family—rather the opposite. Family solidarity is still generally construed as valuable and irreplaceable, even at high levels. There is more suspicion towards state or extra-familial institutions. Among ordinary people, there is close contact with members of the family of origin long after marriage, and support for adult children as well as a tendency for grown-up children to live at home.

Due to European Union hegemony, the language and assumptions of the anti-family movement are now appearing in Italian debates. The antipathy to the family from European authorities that now bears down upon Italian familialism was well demonstrated by the onslaught in October 2004 against Rocco Buttiglione, chosen by Jose Manuel Barroso, president of the European Commission, as his commissioner for justice. Mr Buttiglione's offence was to declare his support for marriage, to say that children do better with two parents than one— something empirically verifiable by all evidence on family outcomes—and to describe homosexuality as a sin, but not a crime and no reason for discrimination. So great was the outrage caused by these remarks—which would have seemed no more than common knowledge a generation before—that members of the European Parliament from all parties threatened to cause a constitutional crisis by voting down the whole Commission. 'Kick him out', demanded Matthew Parris in *The Times*, claiming he had been 'insulted'. Anti-Christian discrimination was 'now in order': we must not 'tolerate religious superstition', even if it involved plunging 'the EU into crisis'.[5]

It might be surmised that Italy has not developed much in the way of family policy, or family-benefiting measures, because these were not necessary. In Western Europe and Anglophone nations, family building has long been based on living standard criteria. Increasingly, it became necessary to have a certain living standard (including, not least, independent housing) before having children. Holding or acquiring the living standard meant, first, delayed (or no) marriage, and then various forms of family limitation, or birth control. Holding back from reproduction also enabled couples' standard of living to expand, so that material growth was not swallowed up in reproduction. Reproducing at the subsistence margin, or without acquiring (and being able to hold) a certain standard of living came to be regarded as backward, feckless and reprehensible. This living standard is continually rising, so that children compete with (and need) more and more desirable goods.

Italy has entered the demographic transition to low birth rates sharply and very lately, compared with other countries whose birth rates fell much earlier and more gradually. In part, this may be attributed to the slow process of industrial development, followed by a delayed contraceptive revolution and the prevalence of traditional patterns of life favouring large families or unrestricted births. Southern European countries and Ireland have seen massive development within a short space of time. Their people want luxuries too—the right furnishings, cars, marble floors, etc. Rapid economic development has meant Italians entering the consumer society where other attractions not only compete with offspring, but a certain standard of living is felt to be necessary for children themselves. Women's participation in the labour market has accelerated since the 1980s, even if it is still low. The proportion of people complaining that they do not have a sufficient standard of living (e.g. with the ability to heat their home properly, entertain, and buy new furniture and clothes) is far higher in Southern countries than in the North. This rising awareness of one's deprivation *vis-à-vis* others suggests that birth rates have further to fall.

> ... the postponement of family formation and low fertility have become intrinsic, structural factors, in a certain sense implicit in the membership of a modern society. Why should young people study less? Why should young people get married and have children before they gain security and stability regarding education, employment and affective relationships? These aspects are part of a

package of irreversible conquests in an advanced society, which from the demographic point of view involve the postponement of the stages of adult life and an increasingly significant concentration of all the events relevant from a demographic point of view for setting up a family.[6]

Elsewhere, various devices developed over time to compensate people for the costs of child-rearing (horizontal equity measures). These ensured that people with children could retain their position or parity in society—otherwise there would be no children or not enough, since children will always undercut affluence and competitiveness. Such family benefits to ensure a sufficient quantity and quality of children did not develop in Southern countries, not least because they did not have to. They were not relevant to the reproductive or family building patterns, where there were plenty of children. Sentiment and morality, as well as the value of children (economic and otherwise) to the family, kept birth rates up. The extended family and the prevalence of the small industrial or artisan firm based in large measure on family labour, had no parallel in the rest of Europe, or had not for a very long time.

The revolution in modern contraception was long delayed in Catholic Europe. (The ban on contraception was only removed in Spain in 1979.) Once it came, it facilitated a major decline in fertility, as people in Southern European countries got hold of efficient contraception and used the savings to surround themselves with possessions, as people elsewhere had been doing for a long time. Pro-natalist beliefs and norms (reinforced by religion) crumbled, as the ethos of affluence and accumulation took hold—joined to attitudes towards children and marriage as choices, rather than inevitabilities. Birth rates were bound to plummet, since the transition was made suddenly in a society that had made little provision for protecting family living standards from the burden of children. As the Minister for Social Affairs observed in 1994, 'as regards the taxation of family incomes, our country seems to have contributed to the pursuit of... a demographic policy aimed at reducing the size of the family unit, which has fallen in the past 40 years from four to 2.8 members'.[7]

The 'iron triangle of sexuality, economic independence and family formation has been torn apart', in Italy as elsewhere, so that the things that used to go with family formation, such as being an independent citizen, earning money, having your home and having social permission for sex, are no longer dependent upon marriage/parenthood.[8]

It seems that norms and values changed remarkably quickly in Catholic countries. Over the 1980s the proportion of adults agreeing that having children was essential to a woman's identity and well-being fell to 50 per cent in Mexico, Argentina, Italy, Spain, Belgium, and Germany. It was only 25 per cent in the USA, Britain, Canada, Netherlands, Norway, Sweden, and Finland.[9]

However, the gap between desired and observed fertility is higher in countries where fertility rates are lowest (Japan, Italy and Spain), except for Sweden, which has a relatively high fertility rate, but a big gap between actual and desired fertility. In Italy, desired family size is almost a half as large again as attained fertility. Obviously, the later that family formation starts, the stronger the chances of not getting to the desired number of children, if only because of falling fertility and health problems. Many second, third or fourth children are wished for by women, but not born.[10]

Once reproduction becomes based on living-standard criteria, this does not shift, except to make children ever more 'expensive' in terms of other desirable goods, and the opportunity costs they impose in terms of the lost market remuneration of their carers. As the Italian family still provides social protection, while not being able to count on much relief and services, this tends to reinforce low birth and marriage rates.

Italians are also using older methods of family planning—in particular delayed marriage. Uncertain prospects for many young men, housing costs and difficulties, and the movement towards living standards based on double incomes as more women enter the labour market, tip the economic balance against prospective parents. Youth unemployment has been high and, as elsewhere, young people are likely to postpone marriage until they have secure employment. In Southern Italy, one in three 15-24 year olds were unemployed in the late 1990s, and in some areas the rate reached 50-60 per cent.

The share of young people not in education and not employed was around 30 per cent overall even in the 20-24 year old age group (compared with an OECD average of around 18 per cent in the late 1990s and with ten per cent in Austria and Holland).

Italy, along with Portugal, Spain and Greece, has a large percentage of young people, of both sexes, with low educational attainment. Paradoxically, it also has one of the highest university education enrolments in the world, but many do not complete their studies. One in four does not enrol in the second year, and with a tendency to the continued extension and prolongation of education, a third or more students in the 20-23 age group do not envisage concluding their studies in the next five years. Universities encourage and tolerate people staying on for long periods, with students taking an average of six to seven years to complete a degree with a given duration of three or four years. Unless they drop out in the meantime, graduation is at age 26-7, with many students getting their degree when they are over 30. For many young adults, university acts as a 'parking space' where they can wait until they find a job, or want to find a job. In Italy, unemployment rates for graduates were 27.3 per cent for those aged 25-29 in 1999, while the OECD average was 8.1 per cent.

The pool of marriageable men, and therefore couple formation, not only decreases when male unemployment increases and male earnings decline, but also when women become more educated and qualified. By the 1990s, women's enrolments in higher education outnumbered those of men in Greece, Italy, Portugal and Spain.[11] Women's education and earnings reduce the economic need to marry early and allows them to take longer finding a suitable spouse. But as women still seek to 'marry up', this also means that the pool of marriageable men with the same or better professional status is severely reduced as women become as, or more, qualified.[12] The marriage squeeze on men, particularly obvious in countries where a large cohort entered collapsing labour markets in the 1980s, may be being followed by a marriage squeeze on women in many societies. This is driven by higher levels of female education and increased labour force participation. With a relative oversupply of women, men will also be less inclined to marry, particularly when non-marriage means increasing access to uncommitted sex and convenient live-in arrangements— encouraged by female competition for eligible men.[13]

While cohabitation has proceeded apace in central and Northern European societies, with children often now born into cohabitations (particularly first-born children), this is a process hardly begun in Southern states, like Spain and Italy. In Greece and Portugal, cohabitation is low because marriage is high. In Italy and Spain, cohabitation is low because people are not forming unions at all.[14] In central and Northern Europe, the fall of nuptiality is associated with the lower value put on marriage and the decision to cohabit without being married, so that leaving the parental home has been disassociated from family formation and has become a period of living alone or as a childless couple. In Italy and Spain, the family and marriage have, if anything, gained in importance for young people over recent times. They do not reject marriage or procreation, but want to put them off until they have reached the targets that enable them to face these roles with greater equanimity and responsibility, involving having jobs, their own property, nice decor, and no aged parents who need looking after.[15]

In the meantime, Hotel Mama takes the urgency out of setting up an independent household. It is advantageous for young people to live at home, avoiding housing costs, but enjoying the services provided and using earnings for holidays, cars and other personal consumption. Extended singledom proceeds in the absence of 'transitional' states; living alone as much as cohabitating. More than in other Southern nations, Italian young people remain in the parental home for long periods and this has been steadily increasing, as 33.2 per cent of those aged 25-34 stayed at home in 1993, up from 22.4 per cent in 1983. While, in Northern European countries, it is young people with a lower educational level who tend to stay on longer with their parents, in the Mediterranean, this reverses, so that it is the young people aged 16-30 with higher educational qualifications who stay home. In Italy, 55.7 per cent of those with a compulsory school qualification live with their parents, at the next level it is 70.3 per cent and 71.2 per cent for those with the highest level of education in the late 1990s. Indeed, there is a tendency to cling to the status of student, even where young people have a steady job or expect one in the near future.

Families also provide financial help. When a Eurobarometer study asked young people aged 15-24 where they got most of their money from, 67.5 per cent in Italy said their family, compared to an EU average of 45 per cent (17.4 per cent in the UK and 37.8 per cent in Germany). In Southern European countries, the family's role in supporting young people is very heavy, and the state's almost non-existent, while the state's help often surpasses that of the family in Nordic countries. The money is in the family, or with the older people. If the family can afford it, their children have relative financial independence, or a basic income which guarantees the young adult a satisfactory amount of buying power. Such generational integration often leaves young Italians and Spaniards with a higher standard of living in relation to that of older people, compared with their peers in Northern countries. However, the proportion of unemployed young people in otherwise workless households is relatively low in Southern Europe, compared with the UK, with its high proportions of jobless lone parents and families living on social assistance. Within unions, it is increases in female wages which are estimated to have played a major role in the strong decline in the fertility rate in Italy.[16] Even a small change in wages (one per cent), can cause a decrease of 2.5 per cent in the probability of having children and an increase of 2.8 per cent in the probability of working. Research provides no support for the idea that the low birth rate is a consequence of Italian women's distaste for motherhood and enthusiasm for market work. The peculiarities of the Italian labour market force all-or-nothing choices on Italian women, to a greater extent than in other industrialised countries. To gain the benefits of a higher wage, women not only have to enter the labour market, but have to commit most of their time to market work, with little time left over for other activities, including childcare. Almost all female employment is in full-time jobs, unlike Northern Europe, as shown in Table 1 (p. 7). Everywhere else, part-time work has increased enormously, and women have taken the vast majority of part-time jobs, since they can fit these around their main responsibility for the family. Italian women's employment rates are the lowest of OECD countries, at 52.8 per cent for childless women aged 24-54 in 2000, 42.4 per cent for those with two children (only Luxembourg was lower), and 46.9 per cent for those with a child under six years of age (in 2001). This compares with 55.5 per cent with a child under six in the UK. It is unsurprising, therefore, that Italy, along with Greece and Spain, also has one of the biggest gender gaps in employment between men and women in OECD countries—33.9 per cent, compared with the average gap of 18.6 per cent.[17] However, only 25 per cent of Italian working mothers with a child under six worked part-time in 2001, compared with 66.4 per cent in the UK, and only 23.7 per cent of all women workers were part-time, compared with 40.8 per cent in the UK. Most women part-time workers do not want to work full time, and many full-timers want part-time work, and it is unlikely to be much different in Italy. Southern European countries have not yet developed the substantial workforces of permanent part-time jobs that have been established in Northern Europe. Unlike Sweden and the UK, there are few part-time opportunities, and men's share of domestic labour is the lowest in the developed world.

If anything, the situation has been exacerbated by employment legislation which offers superior terms and conditions to pregnant women or those who have recently given birth or are breast-feeding. This probably discourages employers from taking on mothers and reinforces the all-or-nothing decision of Italian women. High rates of unemployment in Italy might also discourage women from ever leaving the labour market. Continuous attachment to the labour market is correlated with lower realised fertility in Italy, as is the case worldwide.

Unlike other Western societies, countries like Italy, Japan and Spain have had low levels of female headship, with less than five per cent of all families with children headed by a lone mother in the 1990s. The evolution of the prevalence of lone mothers over time has been quite different across the 17 countries surveyed from the Luxembourg Income Study (LIS) to examine the trends in lone motherhood during the 1980s and 1990s.[18] Twelve out of 17 countries experienced an increase, the largest in France (7.2 percentage points from 1984 to 1994). The largest decrease in this period was in Italy (0.54 percentage points from 1991 to 1995). In Italy, 1.7 per cent of women aged 18-60 were lone mothers in 1994-98 (with a child under 18), the lowest prevalence. In the UK, it was 12.8 per cent.

Births have shifted little outside of marriage in Italy, even given that the unwed proportion rose from 6.5 per cent of all births in 1990 to 9.16 per cent by 2000. Most lone parenthood is still created by divorce, separation and widowhood, rather than unwed births—not least because cohabitation is still so low and teen birth rates are tiny. In Italy only 14 per cent of all single mothers had never been married (compared with 71 per cent in Denmark and 63 per cent in France in the mid-1990s). In turn, only one per cent of never-married mothers in Italy were cohabiting, compared with 40 per cent in Denmark and 21 per cent in the USA.

Legislation was introduced in 1970 allowing for divorce as a solution to the irreversible breakdown of marriage. In 1975, a reform of family law left in force two forms of legal separation, one by mutual consent and one granted on the basis that the 'continuation of cohabitation' would be 'intolerable'. Either party, not just the 'innocent party', may request a separation. Separation has to be established before divorce is possible.

There is compulsory counselling and, while divorce is becoming more common, it still carries a stigma in many parts of the country. The stigma is rapidly diminishing, however. Separation applies for two years, after which the couple go before the Italian equivalent of a JP, who tries to find grounds for reconciliation. Divorce is very expensive and costs are the main break on its increase. Many separated couples continue to live under the same roof because of housing costs—the same reason that marriages are becoming rarer and later.

However, given the European-driven emphasis on acceptance of 'new family forms', help for lone parenthood is increasing. In international terms, the UK offers a medium-high level of assistance to lone mothers, and the highest for Anglophone societies, with a strong preference for this type of family embedded in its social policy. In Italy, not only have (means-tested) family allowances been very low, or about five per cent of median equivalent disposable income, but, between 1988 and 1994, their real value actually decreased by 38 per cent. In 1991, the level of benefits stood at 3.3 per cent and 2.6 per cent of average male manufacturing earnings (AMEM), for two- and one-parent families respectively. But while the level was lower for lone parents, in the late 1990s there was a substantial increase in the level for lone-parent families, while the rate for two-parent families hardly changed,. Rising to 9.8 per cent (AMEM) for lone parents, it now outstripped the rate for two-parent families.

3. Problems with Family Policy

There is far less research information on Italy, because one-parent families, and all other innovations in family structure, are still too rare to be studied reliably. For Italy, we have to be content with more basic information on trends in family composition and well-being.

Italy is characterised by a low level of support for families and a high level of support for pensioners. This is self-reinforcing. The more pensioners there are, the more they get—so there is less and less available for families, so births fall further. The increase in the percentage of elderly people (over 65) in relation to the working part of the population is already greatest for Italy, which became the first country where old people outnumber the young. In 2000, the working-age/elderly ratio in Italy was almost 2:1. It will be 1:1 by 2030, so that every working-age person will have a pensioner to support. In 1990, the accumulated pension rights of over-25s in Italy already amounted to 157 per cent of GDP. In 2030, they will rise to 207 per cent—the highest in Europe.[19]

Pension payments made up more than 70 per cent of Italian social expenditure by the late 1990s. Other expenditure sections must make do with the leftovers. Expenditure on pensions rose from ten per cent of GDP to nearly 16 per cent in 1995 (compared with under one per cent for families), in spite of attempts at reform in 1992 and 1995. Even so, many pensions are low. In the 1990s, economic problems and public sector deficits militated against improving help for families. As elsewhere, benefits for families came last, and were the easiest to sacrifice.

The Italian experience illustrates David Thomson's thesis that the decline of family policy from the 1970s is attributable to processes inherent in modern welfare states, although his thesis was formulated to explain developments in the UK, Australia and New Zealand.[20] Initially, welfare provisions purported to treat all people equally, upon the trust that one generation would cede its place to a second, and so on, if the exchange was not to break down. But welfare states lead to the tragedy of the commons. Common land belongs to no-one, so no-one has an incentive to protect it. Instead, it is in everyone's interest to pasture another cow before someone else gets there. Result: destruction. Mass pooling robs 'us of an identifiable community with whose resources each elector must act responsibly'. Instead it 'promises anonymity and dims the sense that an individual's actions necessarily have consequences for others'.[21] This 'can be seen as the inexorable working out of the logic of our particular forms of collective action. Idealism and public spirit must in time be corrupted into self-centredness, not because the welfare state experiment has failed or gone off the tracks somewhere along the way, but because it has succeeded.'[22]

What is pertinent here is that all policies will shift resources from one group to another, affecting the life chances of individuals. From the 1930s to the 1960s, they worked to assist young adults and their children. Afterwards, they benefited elderly people. This has happened in Italy, an otherwise 'family-friendly' society and to a pronounced degree, as well as in the relatively child-averse UK, and underlines how much these tendencies in modern welfare states develop relatively autonomously of culture.

The Italian experience also acts as a refutation of well-worn claims that the problems of younger generations are owed to the ways that social policy has simply failed to catch up with a popular retreat from family life. This, it is claimed, puts women and children at risk of poverty, because high divorce rates, lower fertility rates, the prevalence of lone-parent families, and greater female participation in the workplace, have moved society away from the single breadwinner in a nuclear family that the welfare state was allegedly designed to prop up. Yet Italy has seen no major movement towards 'alternative' families, or radical new lifestyles. Even in the Anglophone world, only some of the slump and delay in marriage and marital births can be explained by the willingness to have children out of wedlock, despite all the advocacy for this as a newly invented 'family form'.

Italy typifies and leads the way in which Europe can be characterised as a place where 'rich old people [are] supported by the labour of poor young people. No wonder nobody wants to have children.'[23] While the practice may be outlawed by the European equal opportunities legislation, the sentiment lives on that fathers must have preference over single or childless men and women when it comes to employment and remuneration. As equal opportunities legislation has helped push living standards towards a two-income norm, so young men's marriageability is squeezed on two fronts. In turn, while the welfare system also transfers more to the fathers than to the sons, Italian fathers are happy to keep the sons, as money gets redistributed within families. Indeed, rises in parents' income, whether from earnings or pensions, significantly raises the propensity for children to live at home.[24] As family solidarity networks compensate for the dearth of government help, this reinforces the lack of youth- or family-oriented assistance, with politicians trusting in the family's 'miracle-working powers'.

Young people can be ignored and their condition relegated to the 'limbo of "extended childhood"'.[25]

In all European states, the purchasing power of couples without children is higher than the purchasing power of families. However, the differences between countries are large—being particularly pronounced for Italy, Ireland, the Netherlands and the UK.

While interest-group politics are alive and well elsewhere, Italian politics and public services are particularly given to 'particularism' and 'clientelism', leaving general and long-term interests neglected. While attention is given to specific and corporate interests, families are a general part of the landscape which can be taken for granted, and what they get is residual. As in other areas (the leaning tower of Pisa and the sinking of Venice), family policy has been talked about more than acted upon.

More than elsewhere, the family's living standards have depended heavily on what happens in other policy areas and developments affecting the labour market, services, social security and housing. In the circumstances, it is convenient to believe that since the family is strong, it can look after itself and can take anything fate throws at it. Family solidarity was irreplaceable, so that no intervention, manoeuvre or programme of the state should intervene in family life and family choices; the corollary of this idea was that no action by the state in this field would be likely to succeed in any case.[26] Fortunately: 'Italy is perhaps the only country in Europe which has been able, up to the present, to count on the family, and the work of the family (in particular, of women), as an "inexhaustible" resource on which to unload the consequences of social and economic transformations and the absence of a modern social policy.'[27]

Even before the present counter-cultural 'war over the family', family policy had long been an area replete with dissension in Italy, with vested interests, corporate privileges and ideological conflicts. There is a Catholic bias which says that to provide fiscal relief is an interference in the affairs of the family. We can now add the progressive bias towards fragmentation and 'alternatives'. The tradition of non-interference in the family—which extends to family benefiting measures, not just social service interventions and regulation and control of family relationships—is now running into the emphasis on civil or individual rights by an anti-family movement oriented towards flexibility and 'diversity'. The state is being called upon to promote and protect the rights of individuals within or against the family rather than those of the family unit or marriage as an institution. Eurospeak is very evident in discussions of policy. Where 'women do not have a job', this is ascribed to 'a product of the profound imbalance still prevailing in many countries when it comes to sharing family responsibilities'.[28]

While 'alternative' family forms are much rarer in Italy than elsewhere, the same rhetoric has appeared, claiming that 'the traditional concept of family, taken as the union between a man and a woman founded on marriage—accepted both by the Constitution and the civil code—is nowadays inadequate'.[29] It is apparently 'inadequate' because of bizarre cases like that of a woman who carried a child for a daughter without a uterus. The percentage of births out-of-wedlock, levels of living together outside of marriage and rates of divorce are well below those of the rest of Europe—particularly Northern Europe—although they are closer to Northern European levels in the North of the country compared with the South. However, a strained case is made for 'a greater diversification of family types'. These 'new family models' are apparently 'single parent and one-person families'.[30] Since when was a single person a 'family'?

Several recent policy proposals to support the family have attracted criticism which reflects current perspectives. A bill in 1996 provided for the granting of tax exemptions and reduced mortgages to low-income couples under 32 years of age, living in towns with more than 150,000 inhabitants and who undertook to marry within six months from the presentation of the application. It promised that there would only be a small number of beneficiaries, and excluded cohabitees to get the support of the Catholic hierarchy. The left and liberals hated it for 'surreptitiously following a policy aimed at increasing the birth rate and in favour of marriage'.[31] Italy, like other southern European countries and Ireland, does not recognise consensual unions in law, although some regions have introduced registers for cohabiting couples without granting legal rights.

In the 1990s it was envisaged that a reform of taxation would allow couples to opt for the 'family quotient' (already used in France and Luxembourg) that treats the family, rather than the individual, as the tax unit, and lets people split their combined income in relation to their numbers. It was objected to on grounds that it did not attend to children's interest sufficiently (as with opposition to the married-couples allowance in the UK) and that allowances should be focused on the children (as if they could bring themselves up) as a pretext for avoiding any support for marriage.

Child poverty rates

Poor households are defined as those with an annual net monetary income below 50 per cent of the national average. In Italy, child poverty is still very dependent upon the size, rather than the constitution, of the family. The situation is reminiscent of the UK in the 1960s and 1970s, when large families, or those with three or more children (rather than lone parenthood) typified family poverty. In turn, poverty is exacerbated in families where there is only one income. About three-quarters of poor families are not poor because of unemployment, but because *only one* member has a job or a pension.

In some countries, like the UK, child poverty rates for lone-parent households rise as children age. Italy is one of the countries where poverty rates fall in lone-parent households as children age, from 21 per cent for children under six to 17 per cent for children over six years of age.[32] This probably reflects the parent entering work as the youngest child begins school. Divorced lone mothers are everywhere more likely to work than single lone mothers, and Italian lone mothers are more likely to be divorced or separated or widowed, since the unwed birth rate has been so low compared with the UK.

While it is a phenomenon increasingly prevalent in many advanced societies, Italy displays one of the biggest discrepancies between the percentage of children and the percentage of older people living in households at three poverty thresholds (40, 50 and 60 per cent of the mean), with children consistently and markedly poorer at all levels. The Latin countries, like Spain and Portugal as well as Italy, have high child poverty rates compared with the rates for the aged, as do Anglophone countries. The Scandinavian countries of Denmark, Finland, Norway and Sweden, as well as Belgium, have child poverty rates more in balance or lower than aged poverty rates. The poverty of elderly people is related to the absence or presence of an extended family in Italy, so that the poverty rate for older people rises, especially in the South, when they do not have a family to count on. In total, older people are more likely to be poor in the North, since fewer have an extended family to care for them.

It is Italian households with children who have been more likely to be reporting poor living conditions in terms of being unable to afford a holiday, to meet fuel bills, to eat meat or fish, etc., than households with children elsewhere, with the exceptions of two countries, Ireland and Greece. Poor households are defined as those with an annual net monetary income which is below 50 per cent of the average (or 60 per cent of the median) equivalised annual net monetary income of all households in that country—a relative measure dependent upon living standards in respective countries. Children estimated to be in poverty in Italy amounted to 15.7 per cent in 2000. As expected, the rate rose to 61.1 per cent for children in two-parent households where nobody is working; 23.9 per cent where one parent is working; and went down to 1.6 per cent where there are two workers. In households with a non-working lone parent it is 76.8 per cent and where the parent is working it is 13.4 per cent.[33]

Family measures[34] and child benefits

All EU countries except Greece, Spain and Italy have a system of universal child or family allowances paid regardless of income (although in Greece the means-tested child benefit scheme extends far up the income scale). Italian means-tested family allowances are among the lowest in Europe. Originally, there was one family allowance for dependent family members (spouses, children, students, the elderly and the disabled). In the 1960s and 1970s, family allowances were still worth between five and ten per cent of a worker's wage for a couple with two or three children. Between 1980 and 1990, the value of family allowances fell by nearly ten per cent. By 1990, Italy was third from last on the European scale of public spending for family allowances as a percentage of GNP (0.6 per cent).[35] A separate index is kept of payments collected from wage-earners and earmarked for family allowances. In 1994, it was found that less than a third was disbursed in family allowances, the rest having been used to meet deficits in other areas of social security spending

After 1988, the family allowance ceased to be a universal benefit and became means-tested. The right to family allowances was limited to the families of wage-earners and pensioners, disqualifying other categories of citizens. The number of beneficiaries declined dramatically. As it was also not index-linked, it had lost almost 40 per cent of purchasing power by 1996. Wages or pensions must be 70 per cent of total household taxable income to qualify, thus disqualifying those with unearned income, or living on savings. While the family allowance is increased for the numbers of children, it is also reduced for each brother, sister or nephew of the household head residing with the couple.

Family taxation

Mediterranean countries are more likely to channel redistribution towards families through the tax system than through family allowances or other benefits. Italy uses independent taxation of couples, but with a small tax allowance for children and dependent spouses. The dependent spouse credit reduces up the income scale for the supporting relative.[36] By the late 1990s, there was an uprating for the income tax deduction for dependent spouses at the same time as the family allowance was uprated.[37]

Tax systems which offer concessions to couples tend to disproportionately benefit families with children, especially those in the middle of the income distribution.[38] However, this detracts little from Italy's family policy as largely one of low-income support measures for the costs of children. A child's tax credit is split 50/50 between the parents. Provided a spouse's income did not exceed €2,841 in 2002, an income-related tax credit is available. For a lone parent, the credit for the first child is the same as for dependent spouses. The child's tax credit is also granted for other dependents—e.g. parents, parents-in-law, and is similarly means-tested. Alimony payments are tax deductible. There is a variety of other tax allowances, including one for mortgage loan interest, life insurance premiums and university expenses. Employee contributions are the same for all workers, irrespective of dependencies.

In the late 1990s, there was an uprating of the family allowance or benefit, with double the number of beneficiaries envisaged, which also increased the value more for a lone parent (by about 25 per cent). On an annual income of €11,697, the monthly benefit became €250.48 for a four-person (two-child) family. On an income between €28,358 and €31,133, the monthly benefit became €38.73, to cease when income is over €45,017. However, if one family member is handicapped, entitlement is increased by a rise in the ceiling of family income by €8,001. Birth or maternity grants became available for third and subsequent children (and for a second child in 2004).[39]

By the end of the century, the 'child package' was relatively generous in the UK, France, Luxembourg, Belgium, and Sweden for low-income, one-earner families (lone or couple). For Spain, Greece and Italy the restricted package mainly helped families at very low income levels. By the time a couple plus two children hit income of one-and-a-half times the average, the income package started turning negative due to education and health costs. Spending on family cash benefits and services rose to one per cent of GDP by 2001 (compared to

2.2 in UK).[40] Generally, the tax take dropped by more than eight points between 1996 and 2003.

By 2003/4, single Italians with no children at the average wage paid nearly 28 per cent of their income in income tax and social security contributions. A married couple on one wage with two children paid over 15 per cent (taking cash benefits into consideration). The tax burden with an average and a secondary wage (of a third of the main wage-earner's income) is slightly less than on one wage. The rate for the UK was over 24 per cent for a single person without children and nearly ten per cent for one-earner family and two children.[41] At one-and-two-thirds the average wage level, a single Italian paid taxes of nearly 37 per cent, compared to a married couple with children paying over 21 per cent. The marginal rate of income tax plus employee contributions is relatively high in Italy (given means testing in the tax system), and amounts to over 40 per cent for singles and married couples (with and without children) at average wage levels. This is nothing like the level in the UK, which reaches 70 per cent or more for couples with children.

There are the occasional flamboyant gestures, like that of €1,000 for women having a second child by the end of 2004. Some local authorities are also giving baby bonuses, or high family allowances for a number of years after a birth.

Paying for lone parents

In most countries lone parents are treated more generously than couple-families by the tax/benefit system. The same now applies to Italy, although it has a low ranking internationally when it comes to comparisons with the lone parent's net income and that of married couples with children, while the UK has the highest income for lone parents *vis-a-vis* couples at low and average earning levels. In Italy, at two-thirds of the average wage, a lone parent with two children still made a small positive tax contribution in 2003 compared with more than a 20 per cent top-up in the UK.[42] There are no particular provisions for lone parents—apart from the creeping availability of more tax relief and bigger family allowances, and these depend upon being a worker or a pensioner. There are still allowances in the system for spouses, or for the second adult. There is a social assistance scheme in test phase in various areas, which involves a work check when a child is three years old, as well as help available from social services and charitable bodies to deal with particular problems or crises.

This is part of a patchwork of local policies providing social assistance, usually means-tested and aimed at people in difficulty. Like local baby bonuses, benefits vary widely and may be more or less integrated with those of the local council or health board, or delegated to these authorities.

The lower levels of financial help may be one reason why lone parents are far more likely to be in the labour force than they are in the UK, with 74 per cent employed in 2001, compared to 49 per cent in the UK.

Given the high risk of poverty under such a system, there is a relatively limited amount of visible poverty in comparison with other countries, given the low rate of lone parenthood and high level of support provided by relatives. But then, it has been observed elsewhere that, the more efficient and generous a welfare programme is, the more clients there are and, consequently, the more poverty is discovered and even encouraged.[43]

4. What to Do?

It might seem that it is the attenuated transition to adulthood, created by a number of integrated social and economic factors, that is at the heart of Italy's current demographic dilemma.[44] However, this analysis is a far cry from that of many observers with a more Eurocentric perspective who insist 'that the female employment dimension is the main factor determining fertility levels',[45] or that low fertility is 'a symptom of problems in the family and of a lack of social and cultural adjustment to the emergence of the working mother'.[46] According to femocrats in the European Union, 'family-and-work' is the only medium through which family life can be recognised and supported. Since they opine that there is not enough female employment, policies to promote it must be the main instruments for 'effectively intervening in fertility levels and achieving replacement fertility in Europe'.[47] The prescription is for the adoption of the Nordic, or rather, Swedish model, in Italy as in the UK and everywhere else, with goals of equal outcomes for men and women in the labour market, together with equalisation of their household labour or 'an across the board re-design of gender relations'[48] and institutional childcare.

It is taken for granted that the 'majority of women want to participate in the labour force and share care and domestic work with their partners; they are increasingly aspiring towards an equal gender division in family and household tasks'.[49] The confident prediction is that if 'policy makers enable women to better reconcile work and family life and men take on a greater share of the household tasks, couples wanting to have children will realise their plans more readily.' Such 'modernised gender relationships' and the 'exercise of a pro-natalist choice and the creation of a better environment for children will only be possible through modernised family polices and alternative childcare policies...'[50] At the same time, 'society must attempt to equalise the economic outcomes for different family configurations', presumably meaning more subsidisation of lone parents, although it is not at all clear how a failure to support lone parents is holding down the Italian birth rate.[51] However, it is not obvious that 'we are living in societies where men and women want continuous involvement in their career', so that if they cannot 'we will probably run the risk that women will choose not to have children or have them very late in life'.[52] Most people have jobs, not careers, and such statements are made by professional elites who want to recast the world in their own image; one where every woman is a Patricia Hewitt doppelganger.

4

Britain: The Worst of All Worlds?

The main changes in family[1] structure in recent decades are:

- fewer children, with delayed childbearing and increasing childlessness;
- declining marriage, more divorces and rising cohabitation;
- a growth of lone motherhood, first from divorce and then from non-marriage, with a concomitant decline in adoption;
- a growth in step-families and multiple, or sequential, relationships;
- decline in extended families and multi-family households, with overall fewer kin;
- a growth in living alone;
- more elderly people due to population aging;
- the highest teenage pregnancy rate in western Europe, which shows little sign of falling;

The policy background

When income tax was first instituted at the end of the eighteenth century, there were allowances for dependents, which fell into disuse and then were revived in 1906 as part of a pro-family package. At the turn of the twentieth century there was concern at mortality and morbidity among children as the birth rate declined, and from 1890, the health and welfare of mothers gained increasing attention. A four-week unpaid leave for working mothers was introduced in 1895. Training and certification of midwives was introduced in 1902. Free school meals and medical inspections of school children arrived in 1906 and 1907. In 1914 the government decided to grant local authorities matching funds to establish child and maternal welfare services, and in 1918 the initiative was reinforced by the Maternity and Child Welfare Act. These provisions were aimed at improving the health of expectant and nursing mothers and young children, with hospital services for children under five, maternity hospitals, and homes for the children of widowed and deserted mothers. Separation allowances for widows and orphans of soldiers were introduced in 1914. In the background was the tacit assumption that men were expected to earn a 'living wage' or 'family wage' — or one sufficient to keep a wife and children at a tolerable standard of living. Trade unions bargained on this basis.

The post-Second-World-War world was the 'golden age' of family policy in the UK, as throughout the English-speaking world. There was an urge to 'reward' the generation that had made the war effort, allied to a conviction about the need for social solidarity to underpin the development of a comprehensive welfare state. Family allowances were the first part of the 'welfare state' package to be introduced in 1943, along with maternity payments.

The 1960s legal watershed

Until very recently, the family was a morally loaded concept embodying an ideal image, or model of relationships, to be supported independently of the numbers approximating to it — although its decline was a cause of concern and reason for action.[2] Family values provided an impetus for those compensatory measures which, in reducing the standard of living penalty and the opportunity costs of childrearing, upheld its status. Similarly, law and morality had been brought to bear on sexual and reproductive behaviour expressly to maintain social cohesion and continuity. As family stability secured the social good, so the 'first function of the marriage law' was to confirm 'and protect the institution of the family as the assumed and approved foundation of society'.[3] Marriage as an institution helped individuals honour the long-term contract by providing support for couples *qua* couples and by imposing social and economic costs on those who dissolved or disrupted their union.

After reaching its apogee by the mid-twentieth century, family policy in the UK is a story of decline and fall. By the end of the last century, it was essentially dead, not least because:

> ... in Westminster the whole subject of family formation is strictly off limits, though families are the building blocks of society and the health of families determines the health of the nation. Marriage, in particular—the one institution which holds families together—is regarded as just one among a range of lifestyle choices, between which it would be invidious to comment.[4]

Instead, the targets of policies that impact on families are poverty and inequality; fostering equal outcomes for women in the labour market; and enhancing the role of the state in child-rearing. With the definition of family stretched to cover virtually any living situation and all transitional states, a great 'diversity of living arrangements and family forms' are constantly proclaimed. However, anyone looking for exotic innovations will be disappointed, since the 'new family forms' amount to 'increased... cohabitation, separation, divorce, lone parenthood, step-families and people living on their own', and 'a greater acknowledgement of same sex relationships'.[5] But whatever is happening, the state is deemed to be powerless when it comes to family trends. Those hostile to marriage and the nuclear family have eagerly turned projections of their virtual demise into prophecies which we are obliged to fulfil. Its friends have taken consolation and refuge from a contentious, painful subject in the same determinism.

Significant changes in legislation occurred in the 1960s. The Family Planning Act 1967 enabled local authorities to provide free contraceptive advice and supplies irrespective of marital status. The Abortion Act 1967 allowed abortion if the continuation of the pregnancy would involve greater risk to the mental and physical health of the mother than if the pregnancy were terminated. Most importantly, the 1969 Divorce Reform Act had brought in divorce on the sole ground that the marriage had 'irretrievably' broken down. That the marriage had reached such a stage soon became dependent upon the subjective judgment of the parties, with no external standards applied and no investigation conducted. Even if only one partner thought that the marriage had 'irretrievably broken down' then it had — allowing unilateral, no-fault divorce.

Deterministic and naturalistic perspectives were popular in the 1960s and went with the prestige accorded to social science, and with a belief that human affairs might be ordered according to expert knowledge. Those who accepted that the law elucidated and upheld standards of behaviour and that marriage was a public, legally defined institution where the law, and not the parties, established the rules of entry and membership were characterised as 'institutionalists' sacrificing individuals to absurd abstract entities and rules which had no concrete existence in the material world. Their opponents were progressive 'abolitionists' who saw 'divorce as neither good or bad... judged in much the same way as one judges the decision to resign from a job', with marriage a private matter, which only served the interests of those directly involved.[6]

Many opposed to divorce or lukewarm about this (for example the churches) were taken in by the experts' claims that marriages died natural deaths and that it was possible to identify the corpses. In practice, no one had the slightest idea of how to tell a 'dead' marriage from the living thing. In spite of this, determinist/naturalist explanations overcame anxieties that a change in the law making divorce easier might encourage this, by putting 'family breakdown' outside of human control. It cannot be exaggerated how much notions that there were a fixed number of 'hollow shells', and that arrangements like laws were incapable of affecting behaviour, provided comfort for those who had hitherto been of the persuasion that the law constrained and influenced human behaviour. Now all the law could do was to recognise what had already happened in nature. Reform, for the 'abolitionists':

> ...would inevitably result in at least a temporary, and probably large, increase in the number of divorces. Such a rise in the divorce rate would neither stimulate nor reflect any change in marriage breakdowns; it would represent the *de jure* dissolution of marriages which had existed *de facto* only in text-books of theology and in legal theory.[7]

It was argued that the stability and prestige of marriage would actually be promoted by cutting out the dead wood, or all those nasty 'hollow shells'. Then there would be a reduction in the out-of-wedlock birth rate and cohabitation, since all the 'hole in the corner' unions could be formalised. This perspective is with us still in claims that policy, incentives and disincentives, example and suggestions, cannot influence family trends. Insofar as children were concerned, a divorce that benefited the parents, benefited the children, who would have a 'second chance':

> 'Institutionalists' are forced by their presuppositions to assert the benefits to children of maintaining homes intact whatever the relations between parents. The weight of informed opinion is against them, as is the simple consideration curiously ignored by all witnesses. As some two-thirds of all divorced persons may marry again, the chances that a child of divorced parents may achieve emotional security in a new home are high. The effects of divorce on children, though grievous, are frequently exaggerated.[8]

The reliance on 'selected statistics and works of social science'—principally McGregor's *Divorce in England*[9]— 'led to wholly inaccurate predictions about the effect of the Divorce Reform Act 1969'.[10] However, while McGregor had maintained that divorce law would have no effect on the rates of marriage and divorce (since these were in the manner of natural phenomena beyond the reach of law and human action), he also asserted (along with Barbara Wootton) that people should be free to enter and leave unions at will. From the beginning, determinism mingled with nihilism (as with 'permissive' child rearing and educational policies), where people were both in thrall to forces beyond their control and, it seemed to follow, should be free of all constraints. By implication, there was 'a new principle of divorce after separation at the option of the guilty party'. Once conceded, the 'demand to reduce the length of the separation period must prove irresistible; in law, marriage would come to be a tenancy-at-will'.[11]

As nobody could recognise a 'dead marriage', this depended upon two years' separation with consent from both parties, five years' separation without consent, adultery or unreasonable behaviour as evidence of irretrievable breakdown (subjectively interpreted) not grounds for divorce. However, behaviour could be cited in extreme circumstances, or where it would be 'inequitable to disregard' as a consideration in ancillary proceedings over property or children. The notions that liberalising divorce law only leads to the decent burial of already 'dead' marriages before they do more harm, and that the law has no effect on human behaviour, have been re-hashed every time further changes have been proposed or implemented.

In 1973, a Special Procedure was introduced to let couples divorce without ever appearing in court—the postal divorce. In 1982, the position of children born in and out of marriage was equalised. Further legislation on divorce came in the 1984 Matrimonial and Family Proceedings Act, allowing divorce sooner after marriage, and introducing 'clean break' settlements (which swept away provisos to leave the parties to divorce, insofar as possible, in the same economic position they would be in if the marriage endured), although this was already in place where there was childless marriage. For the first time, a government whip was put upon divorce legislation. While it was talked up as a matter of the greatest urgency and need ('no one can exaggerate the need'), it was said that the Lord Chancellor had been lobbied by men moaning about paying for their ex-wives and children. There was no other pressure for this. The (predictable) effects—of men avoiding payment for children of previous marriages—led to child support legislation in 1991. This established a formula for calculating an absent parent's liability to support children in a move from the courts to an administrative agency. Policy makers were particularly motivated by a wish to raise more contributions from absent fathers to offset the mothers' social security payments. It was changed in 1995 to reduce the burdens on absent fathers and their 'new families'. The Child Support Agency has been generally rendered ineffective by excessive bureaucracy and a terror of doing anything in case of adverse publicity.

There was no public pressure either for the 1995 White Paper *Looking to the Future: Mediation and the Ground for Divorce*.[12] This proposed that the behaviour of the parties would no longer have any relevance to divorce applications. Ostensibly the reason was to take the conflict out of divorce which, it was believed, originated when one or both parties made accusations about behaviour. Without conflict, owed to accusations of fault, divorce would be rendered harmless. The 'proof' of irretrievable breakdown, *de jure* as much as *de facto*, would depend upon nothing more than the claim of the petitioner.

A period of 12 months for 'reflection and consideration' was proposed. It was extended for those with children in the passage of the legislation, along with a number of other speed bumps. A great store was also set for mediation as a way to get the conflict out of divorce, where people would agree on how to split the property and allocate the children. The legislation was never implemented, since trial runs with mediation proved ineffective. In particular, mediation worked against the weaker party and was especially disliked where there had been violence. People wanted lawyers to protect their interests.

Providing for the casualties

Divorce reform transformed the economic as much as the legal approach to family support. Claims that divorce reform would change nothing and even lead to a decrease in lone parenthood were belied by the appointment of the Finer Committee on One Parent Families in the same year as the first major reform. But nobody wanted to notice. As the Finer Committee acknowledged, a process was under way in which courts, churchmen and governments were no longer prepared to uphold standards of sexual morality.[13] These were now matters of personal feelings. It also seemed to follow that it was impossible—or, rather, impermissible—to restrict the freedom to divorce, remarry and reproduce if it meant that these behaviours continued to be rationed by their costs. Under fault-based divorce, costs were largely absorbed by the parties concerned, so society was protected from having to bear them. But now, Finer argued, what had 'to be faced [was] that in a democratic society, which cannot legislate (even if it could enforce) different rules of familial and sexual behaviour depending on the ability to pay for the consequences, the community has to bear much of the cost of broken homes and unmarried motherhood'.[14] While it acknowledged that husbands and fathers had some responsibility, not many could support two or more families or multiple sets of children. To expect the people involved to meet the bill for the 'casualties' created by the exercise of their sexual freedom was to 'impose a stricter standard of familial conduct and sexual morality upon the poor than it demands from others'. Since this could not be tolerated, the costs 'must fall upon public funds'.[15]

If the community permits divorce it must be prepared to meet the inevitable consequences of divorce... Rational reform implies modifications in attitudes towards the consequences of divorce. A marriage creates dependencies; so also its dissolution may create social casualties which confront responsible people with conflicting obligations that cannot be discharged because there is insufficient money to go round. Such casualties must be accepted at least as the temporary responsibility of social policy.[16]

Moreover, as reform had revolutionised attitudes towards the consequences of divorce, the view was firmly rejected that provision for lone parents needed to avoid undermining the institution of marriage. The sweeping away of legal restrictions on the freedom of people to escape from bonds previously defended as essential safeguards for the integrity of marriage as a lifelong union made this irrelevant. As the new public policy affirmed ties of choice, moral connotations no longer attached to various patterns of sexual conduct and their consequences. The only task was to secure the interests of dependent children. As a concomitant of extensive state provision for the 'casualties' of sexual freedom, fiscal support for marriage was withdrawn now that this was in principle a private matter which simply involved the personal choice and satisfaction of the two people involved.

The other side of the state's willingness to dissolve marriages is the collectivisation of the costs. At least, the state picks up the bill for the exercise of sexual choice by the 'needy'.

Finer called for a Guaranteed Maintenance Allowance for all lone parents, means-tested in such a way as only to be extinguished when income reached the level of average male earnings. In addition, they would have extra non-means-tested children's allowances. The argument was that, whatever the level of earnings, it was 'rare for an individual (lone-parent) family not to suffer some measure of financial deprivation, even where the head is able to undertake full-time work at a reasonable wage' and so it was necessary to boost the 'family's income above and beyond the general family support for all families'.[17] However, Finer did not go all the way with the National Council for the Unmarried Mother and her Child (later the National Council for One Parent Families) in asking for a non-means-tested benefit by right for all lone parents to provide them with a basic living standard independently of any maintenance, earnings or other income.

The economic downturn

A decline in family fortunes is detectable by the mid-1960s—the same time as the family came under attack from intellectuals and political activists. There was no impetus to maintain the level of family benefits, so they were allowed to decline in value. There was also an undercurrent of concern about overpopulation, given the very high birth rates of the 1960s. There was a change in mood, as 'all for the kiddies' changed to resentment at the brat plague. Delinquency rose with the high-rise blocks of flats that disfigured the cities in order to increase the housing stock.

The tax threshold tended to fall and, due to a lack of uprating and rising inflation, 'fiscal creep' increased the tax take. For a couple with two children under 11 the direct tax burden was nine per cent of average gross earnings in 1964-5, and 22 per cent in 1994-5. It decreased for the childless and single.

Throughout the Anglo-Saxon world since the mid-1970s, families have become more economically 'vulnerable' to children—although measuring 'poverty' remains a complex and contentious issue, with an underlying problem of definition. Family or child poverty first became noticeable among low-wage, big families. This was a new development, since family poverty was traditionally associated with unemployment. Housing became a growing burden as the proportion of family expenditure allocated to food declined. Moreover, as general support for children in the tax and benefit system fell, and out-of-work assistance rose, this made it pointless for many low-paid providers to work and the 'unemployment trap' appeared. Previously, the floor of wages was above the ceiling of benefits for even low-paid people with children, given family allowance and tax relief.

In 1977, the proportion of the population whose family income after housing costs was below half the national mean was 7.4 per cent. By 1992, the proportion was 24 per cent. This represented a huge rise in the number of children living in relative poverty, or in households whose income is below half the national average. The number of children in UK low-income households peaked in 1996/7. The UK came to have the highest rates of child poverty in the European Union, with those below half average income rising from ten per cent to 34 per cent between 1979 and 1997/8. Poverty rose by 21 percentage points in households with children between 1968 and 1995/6, compared with ten percentage points for childless households. Nearly one in four children lived in families with persistently low incomes, as the proportion of people with relatively low incomes in absolute terms increased after 1979, despite average income growth of over 40 per cent, and a five per cent fall in the number of children. Eleven per cent of all children were in the bottom three income deciles for all seven years between 1991 and 1998. Over a fifth have spent four of the seven years in the bottom three deciles.[18] Patterns in the US, UK, Australia and New Zealand ran parallel; while recessions have helped push more below the thresholds, upturns failed to take as many out.

In the 1960s and 1970s, income for all groups in the UK rose, with the lowest rising fastest. By the 1990s, inequality in the UK was greater than in any country, apart from the US. Only in New Zealand did it grow so rapidly in the 1980s.[19] The share of total income held by the bottom ten per cent of families went down from 4.2 per cent in 1961 to three per cent in 1991, while the share of the top tenth of households increased from 22 to 25 per cent. The ratio of the real income of the top tenth of the population to that of the bottom tenth was roughly 3:1 up to the late 1970s, and then increased to about 4.3:1 by the beginning of the 1990s. However, while decreasing (equivalised disposable) incomes at the bottom get most attention, and the top level of income has increased significantly, the fall for those in the middle of the income distribution has been marked. Such distribution tendencies are now common to many developed countries, as for Australia and New Zealand.[20] The UK had a quarter of children in the poorest fifth of the population and only 14 per cent in the richest in 1994/5. Nearly a half of the richest fifth are singles or couples with two full-time workers (couples without children represent 21 per cent of the whole population, but nearly 40 per cent of the richest fifth).[21] Simultaneous rises in both no-worker and two-worker households are both a cause and effect of increasing family poverty.[22] Increased female labour-force participation increases inequality between households,[23] not least by pushing the incomes of childless couples well ahead of couples with children and sole parents.[24]

Families themselves met rising costs by the traditional means of restricting births (with a decline in family size), and putting more labour onto the market, as the rising economic contribution of wives kept the economic situation of families from declining further. Women had fewer children and therefore more time for paid employment, together with a greater risk of divorce that made labour force attachment a form of personal insurance. The expanded service sector provided greater job availability, with higher wages and more conducive work conditions. Despite the high proportion of women in the workforce and the decline in family size, the economic situation of children worsened. For low-income UK groups, rising female participation slowed inequality growth during the 1980s, but this did not hold for the population as a whole. Here it served to partly offset the narrowing of household earnings in the 1970s and reinforced the widening in the 1980s, with a growing polarisation of 'work-rich' and 'work-poor' households, as the middle thinned.

The growth of lone parenthood

Since 1970, the growth in the proportion of families headed by a lone woman exacerbated problems, and changed the structure of poverty. Lone-parent families have been principally headed by divorced, separated or never-married women, while widowhood became rare. After the rise of divorce, marriage rates fell. To an increasing extent, cohabitation compensated for the decline in marriage, except that cohabitations are much more likely to break up—particularly where there are children.

Given a high profile by pressure groups, lone parenthood came to exemplify family or child poverty by the 1980s, although couples with children were 29 per cent of all people in poverty (on a half-average-income, after housing costs, measure), and lone parent families 23 per cent even in 1999/2000 (or on a 60 per cent of median measure: 32 per cent and 24 per cent), and poor children were split between lone and two-parent families 45 per cent/55 per cent.[25] While a large proportion of lone parents may be poor or on low incomes, they *have not constituted the majority of poor or low-income families or people.*

As a group, people in lone-parent families are proportionally more likely to be in poverty than those in couple-families.[26] Over time, increases in lone-parent households, and so more poverty-prone households, have increased child poverty levels. In 1999/2000, 57 per cent of individuals in lone-parent families were below the half-average-income threshold, compared to 20 per cent in couple-families. Around three in five children with lone parents were poor—or 59 per cent compared to 22 per cent with couples—and the poverty gap between lone and couple-mothers widened overall from the mid-1980s.[27] Moreover, statistics provide a snapshot in time. Persistent poverty, like welfare dependence, is far more a lone-parent than a two-parent phenomenon.

Falling employment

The lone-parent group is not, of course, composed of the same people over time. Employment rates for lone parents fell after the 1970s. In 1981, 55 per cent of lone mothers were working, and 49 per cent by 1989 (70 per cent to 58 per cent for lone fathers). As more were single, rather than divorced, separated or widowed lone parents, they represented more low-ability and poorly-educated girls. In the late 1990s, never-married lone mothers were about four times more likely to be in class IV or V, more than 30 times more likely to be receiving benefits, and almost two-and-a-half times more likely to have no educational qualification than other mothers.[28]

The proportion of lone parents receiving child support payments from non-resident parents fell from 30 per cent in 1989 to 25 per cent in 1999. More than a half assessed through the Child Support Agency do not get full payment. A study by the Social Policy Research Unit at York,[29] based on interviews with non-resident fathers in 1995-6, showed a father was much less likely to pay if unemployed, if he became a father under 20, if he does not provide informal support, if he had not made a formal arrangement for paying, and if he had no contact with the mother. Payment is more likely if the relationship with mother is amicable. When mothers are not receiving income support, the chances of maintenance increase fivefold. However, there may be much undeclared maintenance, particularly where the woman is on income support, since maintenance counts against her benefit if it is not 'on the black'.

Certainly, non-work is likely to mean low income and/or welfare dependency, and the 'workless household' factor is strongly implicated in the risk of child poverty. In the European Union a child living in a household with no working adults is approximately four times more likely to be growing up in poverty than a child in a household with at least one working adult.[30] When men move out of work, women tend to move out with them, or are already not working. Thirty years ago, 92 per cent of British children lived with two parents of whom at least one worked. By 1995-96 the proportion outside such families had risen from eight to 29 per cent, faster than the official unemployment rate and the highest in the European Union.[31] Two out of three working-age households with persistently low incomes, and six out of ten children with persistently low incomes, had no parent in employment.[32]

Measures of 'absolute' poverty in the UK are related to the absence of a parent in any employment, in any family type, and the non-working poor have grown, not only among lone parents. UK research amongst those unemployed in 1995 and 1996 found that the 'partners' of those on means-tested income support were four times as likely to leave work over a six-month period as those whose 'partners' were receiving non-means-tested income support. Analysis suggested that overall slightly under two-fifths of the lower rates of employment amongst the 'partners' of the unemployed was due to the unemployment of the other, rather than other factors, and about a half was due to the potential disincentive effects of means-tested benefits.[33]

Women and the workforce

In the nineteenth century, men's wages and jobs were protected and enhanced as the mainstay of families under the concept of the 'living wage'. In the 1970s, equal pay and opportunity legislation undid this structure and put nothing in its place. More women were entering the workforce anyway and their educational levels were rising. Legislation on equal pay in 1970 was followed by anti-discriminatory (or equal opportunity) laws in 1975. The right to reinstatement after maternity was introduced in 1976, allowing absence of up to 40 weeks with job security.

The expansion of available consumer goods and rising living standards also put pressure on women to earn to afford all these 'extras', so wives now worked between marriage and children, as well as after. The effect was a trend towards living standards based on double incomes. Once women could not 'afford' to forego the advantage of adding to the family income, then they could not 'afford' to leave work. By the 1980s, stagnating and declining male wages and rising male unemployment meant a growing need for a second income. The rise in home ownership was a key factor, locking wives into paid work and fuelling the demand for consumption goods.[34]

The initial response to poverty

The answer to the emerging problem of child or family poverty, and disincentives to employment, in the early 1970s was family income supplement, rather than uprating child tax allowances and/or family allowances. The same movement was evident in housing. Traditionally, public housing was a service for families through the control of rents. This was criticised as wasteful, given that some council tenants had higher paying jobs that others. With 'cars outside' and 21-inch TVs, they could 'afford' proper (i.e. market) rents. Moreover, Labour councils had been keeping rents down to absurdly low levels to favour the 'workers' and buy their votes. So, policy was changed to subsidise 'people, not bricks'. Rents rose and those who could not 'afford' them got a means-tested benefit.

Subsidised people found it was not worthwhile to work. Public housing became increasingly a mark of benefit dependence. By 1996, only a third of families in social housing had any employment.

Taking away family benefits

Opposition to the child tax allowance grew in the 1970s at the same time as income supplements designed to fill the gap between wages and 'needs' were expanded, in a trend away from universalism. This derived in no small part from the notion that tax allowances only went to the 'rich', since you had to have income of a certain level to set them against. To combat child poverty, tax relief was reduced in return for bigger family allowances, which went disproportionately to 'the poor'. There was the idea of progressively increasing the family allowance and taxing it back from 'the rich', even beyond the point where the child tax allowance was eroded away—the 'claw-back'. The 'claw-back' only applied to people with children. Money was taken from families to service their own poor, or to 'help' families. At one point, the minister, David Ennals had to tell a delegation that the policy of the Child Poverty Action Group meant that a man with four or five children would end up leaving the factory gate with negative earnings.[35] Frank Field eventually came to condemn this policy as mistaken; it pulled down families and destroyed incentives, without doing anything for poverty.[36] The more that was taken away from universal entitlements, the poorer families got.

In 1977, the family allowance and tax exemptions were abandoned in favour of a universal child benefit. Initially, it was paid at a lower rate for the first child. From 1978 it was paid at a flat rate for all children, then later raised for the first child. As child benefit was being introduced in 1977, an additional non-means-tested benefit was made available for lone parents, the additional child benefit or one parent benefit in 1981.

In the 1980s, there was renewed emphasis on containing and reducing state expenditure on benefits and services: reducing dependency on benefits and promoting occupational and private benefits. As resource constraints, rising public social expenditures and changing attitudes eroded support for families, sentiment shifted to pensioners. While pensioner benefits expanded, those for families came under pressure as the cause of excessive public spending. Universal benefits were seen as expensive, since they went to everyone in a given category, while selectivity and means-testing were seen as the way to hold down public spending. Child benefit came under the same kind of attacks which had swept away child tax allowances. In further moves way from universalism, and thus from family policy, the core support became means-tested programmes available to those on low incomes.

There seemed to be little appreciation of the dynamic consequences: people are quite capable of manipulating their circumstances to qualify for anything that's available. Strangely, benefit dependency was seen as the uptake of universal allowances, rather than reliance on income-related benefits. The universal child benefit came under particular attack with claims of wastefulness and that the resources could best be targeted at those 'in need'. The value was frozen in 1987 until it was upgraded slightly in 1991.

Dependency grows

Not surprisingly, families began to become more dependent upon income-related transfers from the 1970s. By the century's end, the number claiming Income Support or its earlier equivalent had tripled. Those receiving in-work benefits rose eleven-fold from the advent of family income supplement (or family credit) in 1971 to 1999. The proportion of under-fives whose parents received either income support or family credit stood at nearly 40 per cent, and approached 30 per cent for children aged 12-15.[37] Housing Benefit saw an eight-fold increase in receipt by families with children over the 1990s. This is before a kaleidoscope of constantly changing means-tested benefits brought an estimated 38 per cent of households onto one or another in the new century. Policies based on 'targeting the needy' had vastly increased the numbers on welfare and created new classes of recipients who received means-tested assistance while working, or for their housing costs. Total spending on child-contingent support rose from £10 billion per year in 1975 to £22 billion in 2003 prices, with spending per child rising two-and-a-half-fold.

At the same time, the main clientele of income-related transfers became lone parents. Over a half of all social security spending on families went to lone parents, so that 60 per cent of the increase in spending on child-contingent support, largely means-tested, from the mid-1970s to the end of the century, was caused by changes in the characteristics of households rearing children—such as the increasing proportion with one adult and no one in paid work. This increased expenditure, even allowing for an overall fall in the number of children. Since 2000, increases have owed most to policy changes *per se* as Labour governments aimed to cut child poverty through redistributive means testing. By the new century, 79 per cent of a two-parent family's income was made up of earnings, but only 26 per cent of a lone parent's.[38] Moreover, the proportion of child-contingent support going to lone parents has increased faster than the proportion of children with lone parents.[39] Where a lone parent worked less than 16 hours a week, benefits made up 91 per cent of income. By 2000, 73 per cent of lone parents were receiving family credit or income support: 57 per cent housing benefit and 62 per cent council tax Benefit, compared with 11 per cent, eight per cent and 11 per cent respectively for couples with children.[40] A quarter of lone mothers had been on income support for eight or more years.[41] Payments to cover exceptional needs and social fund loans went mostly to lone parents, and the same applies to the maternity grant, which became means-tested when it was substantially raised in 1987. Three-quarters of English lone parents were housed in the public sector compared to around a fifth of two-parent families.[42]

Dealing with dependency

One way to reduce the disincentive effects of means-tested benefits is to slash entitlements. This defeats the object of targeting the 'needy' and reducing poverty. Another is to provide a 'benefit to get off benefit'. Allowing recipients to earn on the side (a 'disregard'), to have wages subsidies or benefit withdrawn at a slower rate as earnings increase, is a classic move to circumvent the problems of welfare targeting. People are provided with benefits and then with further benefits as incentives to offset the benefits. We get 'broadening target populations', where political expediency adds a new layer to the eligible population. This move is apparent with family income supplement (FIS) as a wage subsidy to stop people going on unemployment benefit. (It had a low take-up rate from two-parent families: a year after its introduction the take-up rate was about 50 per cent, and, by the time it was discontinued in 1988, take-up rates had not altered much.) The hours of work needed to qualify were 30 for couples and 24 for singles. When family credit (FC) came in with the Social Security Act of 1986, the minimum hours were reduced to 24 and it was calculated on net earnings. An award was taken into account in assessing housing benefit (HB) and council tax benefit (CTB). No other means-tested benefit itself had ever been a resource for calculating other means-tested benefits. An award of FC was effectively taxed at 85 per cent until eligibility for HB and/or CTB was exhausted. Owner-occupiers moving from income support to family credit lost mortgage interest reimbursement, and so had added disincentives to work.

Family credit was paid for part-time work of 16 hours to make it friendly to lone parents. Clients then stuck at the high rate paid for minimal earnings and, like income support for the unoccupied, it became a benefit for lone parents. So an extra supplement was paid for working over 20 hours. As so much was withdrawn, and taxes imposed as earning rose, it was still pointless for clients to seek to raise income, especially as benefits were also available for housing costs and local taxes. To reduce withdrawal from over 70 per cent (or 90 per cent if other reliefs were added) to more like 50 per cent, a new working families tax credit (WFTC) was introduced in the late 1990s.

The WFTC extended further up the earnings scale. The extra people brought within scope of the benefit take longer to earn their way out. Subsidies for part-time work that encourage people to get a job may *discourage* recipients from improving their skills or seeking promotion, and so increasing their long-term earnings capacity.[43] It was estimated that nearly a half of all families receiving the US equivalent earned income tax credit (EITC) would have been better off without the subsidy because they have less in total as a result of working fewer hours. This also discourages family formation, since subsidy levels at any level of gross income are the same for one- and two-parent families.

By May 2001, 2.5 million children were in families receiving WFTC awards. Of these 51 per cent were lone-parent families. In the late 1990s, income transfer systems became increasingly complex, and in the new century they were always in a state of transition and revision.

The steady increase in the number of families where no one is in paid work increasingly focused government attention on the work issue. But making lone parents 'self-sufficient' usually involves shifting them from one set of benefits to another. Instead of being housewife and full-time mother paid by the subsidising state, she becomes a secondary or supplementary earner to this primary provider. A lone parent is benefit-dependent in, as well as out of, work in that she cannot earn enough to cover the costs of childcare, while supporting herself and her children.[44] Instead of reducing the fiscal cost of income support by the full amount of benefit that is no longer being paid, part of the cost is simply shifted from income support programmes to the tax credit programmes. Many who move into employment will be equipped only to carry out low-skilled work, which means both that they will command low wages and that their prospects of income growth are low.

It is fantasy to expect resources to be 'freed up' from programmes for getting lone mothers to work. Indeed, while the supposed 'gains' from investing in mother's work and childcare were a staple of reports and discussions in this field in the 1990s, these claims seem to have died away in the 2000s. Either way the state has come to provide role substitution, and endeavours to make up financially for the lack of a second parent. It is blatantly obvious why a lone parent is not self sufficient—there is only person trying to do the work of two, with only one earner in the family who also has to double up to provide care.

The low ability of many welfare mothers does not bode well for raising wages. In general, the effectiveness of training or work experience for dependent groups is low,[45] particularly given its expense and the problem of matching with projected job requirements. If lack of 'high quality, low-cost childcare' and low educational qualifications are two of the more significant barriers to self-reliance for lone parents, then 'high quality, low-cost childcare' is a contradiction in terms. Its expense (even if the personnel could be found to provide it) would outweigh the worth of the mothers' labour elsewhere.

As an increasingly complex and cumbersome tax/benefit system strove to reduce both poverty and work disincentives, lone parents were offered an extra £40 per week for a year in the December 2004 budget if they returned to work at all. Those on minimum wages effectively earn £12 per hour. Since fewer no-work households had moved over the poverty line, the government answered the call from the poverty lobby for substantially increased benefits to achieve 'security for those who cannot work'. The link was broken between receiving tax credits and working—a somewhat questionable move in the face of indications that workless households might be on the rise again. The 'families' bit of the working families tax credit was separated off as the child tax credit and paid irrespective of employment. By 2004/5, a non-working parent would receive credits of £3,800 per year for two children and £5,430 for three on top of income support and other benefits, raising tax/benefit income to over £11,000. And, with a working families tax credit split off from the child tax credit, there is no reason left why childless people cannot claim in-work benefits, so the state has acquired another role in subsidising low-paid workers without children. Yet, the requirement to pay income tax has never reached so low down the income scale. Millions of people who earn less than half the national average pay income tax, and on amounts well below subsistence (in 2004/05 the threshold was £4,745).

The concerns

At the beginning of the twenty-first century, concern about poverty is the driving force in British social policy, followed by the concern with vertical inequities, not horizontal inequalities between those with and without the cost of childrearing. Implicit in the Tory years, this became avowed policy for the Labour government. The government set a specific target to reduce the number of children in low-income households by at least a quarter by 2004/5 compared with 1998/9.

A subsidiary policy to the drive to reduce workless households is the focus on gender equality, or equal outcomes for men and women in jobs and remuneration, as well as in the distribution of care tasks in the home. It is increasingly seen that the answer to closing the pay gap—as women will not push hard enough—is to pull men down, or put trip wires in their path. European Commission directives and recommendations are encouraging convergence in social policy. A key objective of EU equality policy is to achieve 70 per cent female employment rates across the EU in the near future. Reforms will extend maternity pay and allowance from six months to nine months from April 2007, with the intention of moving to 12 months. New fathers will be entitled to six months paternity leave, to be taken in the child's first year of life following the mother's return to work after six months maternity leave. Three months will be paid at the rate of £106 a week, with the money reimbursed by the Treasury. A mother cannot transfer her personal tax allowance to the father, but she will be able to transfer her baby leave, since it is appropriate for fathers to mind babies, but not support families. Predictions are that around two per cent of fathers will initially take advantage of these new 'rights'. Clearly, these developments mirror those in Sweden and, as in Sweden, will be most advantageous to parents working in the expanding bureaucracies, and most disadvantageous to businesses, particularly small businesses. In line with the endorsement of the 'fluid partnership' agenda (see below) the 'daddy' taking paternity leave need not be the actual father of the baby, or even live with it—any 'partner' of the mother will qualify.

The government would like to think that it is pursuing four strategies:

- Redistribution, with the minimum wage, family tax credit, childcare tax credit, child tax credit, child scale rates of income support for children under 11 increased, and the starting rate of tax at ten per cent;
- Employment for all;
- Prevention—with Sure Start for pre-school children, the Social Exclusion Unit, and the strategy to reduce teen motherhood;
- Investment in human capital—in schools, training, the NHS and Childcare Strategy.

There is also a tacit anti-marriage agenda. The abolitionists now dominate or control the organisations, not least the university departments and the government-sponsored quangos or front organisations, dealing with research, advice and policy making in the area of family matters. Hardline feminists like Patricia Hewitt moved into senior government positions and promoted friends like Angela Mason from a homosexual pressure group to head up a Women and Equality Unit. By the late 1990s, the 'scenario opened up by the Labour Government's New Deal and associated tax and benefit changes' coincided 'exactly with the aspirations of gender feminists, now well represented in government, the parliamentary Labour Party and the civil service'.[46] As spelt out by one feminist in 1984:

> The idea of abolishing marriage may sound as attractive as the classical communist call to abolish the family, but such demands are probably as unpopular [with the population] as they are unrealistic. It would be far more effective to undermine the social and legal *need* and support for the marriage contract. This could be achieved by withdrawing the privileges which are currently extended to the married heterosexual couple. Such a move would not entail any punitive sanctions but would simply extend legal recognition to different types of households and relationships, and would end such privileges as the unjustified married man's tax allowance. Illegitimacy would be abolished by realising the right of all women, whether married or single, to give legitimacy to their children. Welfare benefits and tax allowances would also need to be assessed on the basis of individual need or contribution, and not on the basis of family unit...[47]

So, deprive the plant of light and water and cut the roots: then it will wither and die. Most has been accomplished, except Carol Smart's last request, since welfare assessments penalise couples. The 'unjustified married man's [or couple's] tax allowance' was reduced by Kenneth Clarke and removed by Gordon Brown. Civil partnership and other legislation has extended the remaining rights of married couples (inheritance tax exemption, tenancy inheritance, couple adoption, and widow's pensions) to homosexuals. The lone parent is the family form preferred by the tax/benefit system.

The drive for eradication has now reached the Orwellian stage of deleting references to marriage out of the lexicon and from public discourse. Officialdom and business communications must now only refer to 'partners'. Control language and you control thought. Control thought and you control action.[48] Since language not only reflects how people live but guides their behaviour, the aim is the perception and acceptance of a world of provisional, *ad hoc* relationships, where men move around siring and 'parenting' children as 'partners' of essentially lone mothers. Ostensibly, it has been done on the grounds that even a mention of marriage would insult lesbians and gays and stigmatise the unmarried.

> It is envisaged that Government forms currently asking for details of a person's 'marital status' would be altered to read 'civil status'. This category would then include both marriage and civil partnerships and there would be no automatic presumption of someone's sexual orientation. Other requests for personal details would be amended, wherever possible, to ensure that references specific to marriages or civil partnerships were replaced with neutral terms.[49]

Insulting married people by referring to 'partners' does not count.

Apart from 'those of deep religious conviction' no one else is assumed to have much time for marriage. Instead, 'parenthood and parenting may be the fulcrum of their adult lives'.[50] Strange then, that in 2001, 64 per cent of families with dependent children were still married-couple-families (12 per cent were cohabiting couples, and 23 per cent lone parents). Despite this, they are swept aside as an antiquated irrelevance: beneath consideration and fit only for the dustbin of history. We must accept marriage's extinction since the direction of trends is against it, even if this is still a majority behaviour and the aspiration of at least 80 per cent or more of the population. Indeed, there are such 'marked rises in unmarried cohabitation and having children outside of marriage', the co-director at the

Centre for the Study of Social Exclusion argues that this 'raises questions about the hegemony of legal marriage and many of the assumptions on which public policies and even social scientific theories are built'.[51] She opines that marriage is meaningless as a reference point, dead as an institution, and has to be erased from the script and obliterated as irrelevant in research as much as in policy. The implications for research if marriage is an invalid variable is that we cannot (must not?) know how children fare within this, compared to the outcomes for those reared elsewhere. Many studies and databases, including the government's prominent Family and Children Study (FACS), now amalgamate (and thus equate) marital and cohabiting relationships, when it is well known that the two have very different implications and outcomes.

Accusations are sometimes made that governments have sought to 'deny or reverse family change'.[52] On the contrary, UK governments over the last three decades have refused to acknowledge the anti-family nature of policies they have pursued and, particularly of late, have furthered family disintegration, not least by engineering the death of marriage.

Is the policy working?

While the government sought to reduce child poverty (60 per cent of median after-housing costs) by a quarter between 1999 and 2004/5, it fell by around 15 per cent—or 60 per cent of the amount required—by 2002/3.[53] It was down to 28.5 per cent, from 34 per cent at the height in the mid-1990s.[54] It then stalled and, by 2003/04, had fallen by only 100,000 children, with little or no reduction in the number of poor children in two-parent families.

While greater proportions of lone parents are in the lowest income groups, often the poorest people among those out of work, working part-time, or with one earner, are in two-parent families, given that there is no allowance in the benefit system for the cost of another adult. In 2003/4 a lone parent with two children needed £182 per week after taxes and benefits to cross the poverty line, while a couple with two children would have needed £262. A lone parent could have achieved the level on earnings of £82 per week, a couple in social housing would have had to earn £336, or £509 if they paid rent of £132. If lone parents work more than 16 hours a week at the minimum wage, tax credits lift most out of poverty. Of the two million poor children in poor two-parent households, 70 per cent had one or two parents in work. But tax credits do not lift many of these out of poverty. Indeed, as credits reduce at the rate of 37p in the pound for weekly income over £97, even a two-parent family on average earnings would have got only the £10.43 family element (but not the working tax credit or the child element of the child tax credit). Some of these families are likely to have an after-tax-and-benefit income of less than 60 per cent median AHC and so would qualify as poor.

While the government had hoped that most lone parents would rush into the workforce, there was only a 'slight increase in work effort'.[55] Estimates are that reform led to an increase of about seven per cent in the fraction of lone mothers who worked 16 or more hours per week, driven by higher rates of entry and retention in the labour force. The effects were largely limited to mothers with one pre-school child, with virtually no effect on mothers with more and older children,[56] and were probably owed to a higher benefit threshold, a lower taper, and generous childcare credits. Otherwise, the benefit increases for workless lone parents and those working less than 16 hours a week made after 1997 would have largely eliminated the work incentives. A low-income, part-time working lone parent (without childcare costs), saw a rise in real income of seven per cent between 1988 and 1997, 39 per cent between 1997 and 2002 and 11 per cent between 2002 and 2004 and, for a non-working lone parent, this was four per cent, 33 per cent and six per cent.

Unlike the US, where a major factor in joblessness is assumed to be the lack of motivation to find or take work, the belief in the UK is that joblessness results from external barriers: lack of skills, financial or childcare barriers. In one view, people do not work because they have decided against it. In the other, they are 'excluded'. Much is made of how mothers are desperate to join the workforce, when in reality they generally prefer not to work at all when children are young, and then to work part-time when children go to school. Unsurprisingly, mandatory 'must-work' programmes outperform 'may-work' voluntary ones because they make people go to work—whether in Sweden or the US.[57] Work incentives, or training for better jobs, government jobs, childcare, or letting beneficiaries keep benefits when earning, 'do not cause large numbers to rush forward and work who were not working before. That is why most experts abandoned such proposals in America, even on the left.'[58] Schemes designed to raise the prospects of unemployed and low-skilled workers through training and work experience have shown limited success worldwide,[59] particularly given their expense and the problem of matching with projected job requirements. In the UK, the 1999 New Deal for Lone Parents was intended to help lone parents to take jobs and move away from benefits, although there were no penalties for not doing so. It has had little or no effect, with the cost of providing the programme greater than any economic gains from getting parents into work.[60] A previous programme was described as a resounding success for finding jobs for five per cent of lone mothers, far from the 80-90 per cent of unemployed lone mothers purportedly eager to get into work.[61]

More measures, more money, will be needed each year to hold the gains in poverty reduction, let alone make more progress. Changes in poverty are not only the result of policy changes but other economic and social changes. Since poverty grows if a group with a high poverty rate grows in numbers, so encouraging lone parenthood or 'family diversity' and, at the same time, trying to push down poverty, is a very expensive business. Poverty levels also depend both on changes in the incomes of those close to the poverty line and, crucially, changes in median incomes which determine the level of the poverty line. As the poverty line rises over time with real income growth, benefits and tax credits must keep up with a moving target if the rate is to stand still. To reduce child poverty further, the incomes of parents just below the poverty line also need to rise faster than median income, with substantial year-on-year increases in the earnings and/or total state support to low-income families.[62]

Better children?

Deficiencies in children's backgrounds are meant to be countered by the anti-poverty strategy, given beliefs that it is poverty and inequality that disadvantage children, not family structure. If the money does not work, then there are the hopes invested in preventive policies like Sure Start for pre-school children, and the strategy to reduce teen motherhood, along with other avenues to human capital investment like schools, training, the National Childcare Strategy, Early Excellence Centres, Neighbourhood Nurseries and Children's Centres. The 600 children's centres will become 3,500 by 2010 in England alone, with five in each constituency, as they are 'rolled out nationwide'. When free early education for three- and four-year-olds is achieved, this will be extended to two-year-olds. Early education tends to be conflated with baby minding for working mothers. Blair's Chancellor purportedly shares in the belief that the 'life chances of children are critically determined by the care, support and education they receive in the years before five',[63] and that childcare will do a magic fix while mothers work. This wonder remedy is 'critical in supporting social mobility and creating equality of opportunity', which 'benefits society as a whole' and is 'breaking the cycle of disadvantage'.[64]

Unfortunately, the evidence suggests that the difference which extra money *per se* makes to child development is small to non-existent once a rather basic standard of living is reached.[65] Moreover, recent evidence from the British Household Panel Study suggests that the effect of family structure is far more disadvantageous for many young adult outcomes even than parental worklessness.[66] There are doubts as to whether allocating more hours, months or years of early educational provision does incrementally more for child development than simply a few hours a few times a week in the later pre-school years. On the other hand, evidence has mounted that long periods in early group care are associated with later aggressiveness.

The state as parent

Government is not only redefining the family and going into the business of child-rearing and development, it is also increasingly finding ways to regulate it. One person is alone and two people are a crowd or, at least, a group. This is why totalitarian regimes in the twentieth century found themselves on a collision course with families and often preferred promiscuity and lone parenthood, since there are no boundaries and barriers here to state intervention. Anarchy and despotism are two sides of the same coin, and collectivism exists alongside a permissive, hedonistic and solipsistic private morality. T'was ever thus, as expensive and invasive programmes thriving on family disintegration eagerly move in to manage personal life and then address the symptoms of dissolution. A Children's Minister (Margaret Hodge) insists that 'it is not a question of whether we should intrude in family life, but how and when—and we have to constantly remain focused on our purpose: to strengthen and support families so that they can enjoy their opportunities and help provide opportunities for their children'.[67] The 'support' is to ensure that people conform to the government's norms. It is not to help parents achieve what they think is right. They must not be allowed to interfere or prevent young adolescent girls having all the sex they want, so contraceptives and abortions are provided without parental consent or knowledge, well below the legal age of consent to sexual intercourse and the age when parental responsibility ends.

Fatherlessness and the judicial-bureaucratic machinery have grown worldwide together. Since many men are no longer bound to their children through marriage, or even live with them, their contact with children is something imposed, structured and monitored in detail by public bodies. Judicial discretion is itself being taken away in favour of bureaucratic and extra-judicial processes. Parents are increasingly overseen and supervised by officials and supervised by a growing apparatus of quasi judicial family courts, social welfare and civil service agencies.[68] Increasingly intrusive and powerful, these bodies can direct the details of children's upbringing, remove them from home and control the movements, finances and other aspects of the parents' lives. The rights of parents are subordinated to the 'best interests' of the child, as something determined by public bodies and interpreted by court-appointed advocates who 'speak for' children. This is all set to expand due to several developments.

One measure to manage parental behaviour is the legislation on the right to smack. An amendment to the new Children Act (implemented January, 2005) limits the defence of 'reasonable chastisement' to charges of common assault. In practice, it means that if punishment leaves any mark, a charge of actual body harm can be brought, to which 'reasonable chastisement' is no defence. There is great potential here to 'overcharge' and avoid the defence of 'reasonable chastisement' that can be used in cases of common assault. The Attorney General announced that the Director of Public Prosecutions (DPP) intended to amend charging standards in such a way that 'minor assaults by a parent on a child' would normally be charged as assault occasioning actual bodily harm, even where the level of injuries would usually lead to a charge of common assault. This was justified in that an 'assault' on a child by a parent was a 'serious aggravating feature'. A rise in prosecutions for assaulting children might mean that a lot of 'hidden' child abuse was being uncovered. On the other hand an absence of prosecutions may also mean that not enough was being done to stamp out abuse in the family, so that stronger legislation is called for. With the new law being reviewed in a couple of years time, an excuse may be found to push for a complete smacking ban. The consideration also emerges of whether parents can restrict their children's movements, or even restrain them, if accusations of assault or infringement of 'rights' can be made. If a parent grounds a child, can an accusation of false imprisonment be made?

Wales, Northern Ireland, Scotland and England all have children's commissioners. The commissioner has a rights-based function, with scope to take up cases on behalf of individual children, although this is being scaled back somewhat given the potential expense. The commissioner will know what children think and want from special panels or focus groups. How will these be chosen and manipulated? By interested parties anxious to push a particular agenda? Children's rights campaigners eventually want the commissioner to have the right of access to every home. Gathering and assessing children's views is clearly going to be a growth area. The University of Edinburgh offers an MSc covering the way in which children negotiate and interpret their world and how that world treats and mistreats them, as well as how to gather children's views, or rather, interpret or guess what their views are, from interviewing, research or 'participatory' techniques like drawing and drama.

The state must administer discipline if parents are absent, inadequate or hamstrung. Major extensions are planned for parenting contracts and orders, and a wide range of authorities, including anti-social behaviour teams, housing officers, and possibly schools, may be allowed to apply for orders. They are also intended to apply at an earlier age, although how potential miscreants will be identified has hardly been outlined. With more families fragmenting, they cannot rear children adequately while, at the same time, they are wide open to intrusion from external authorities who are now obliged to step in to manage behaviour.

5

Overview and Conclusions

It is difficult to distinguish the separate effects of law and national culture in producing the very different family trends observed in Sweden and Italy. Law and fiscal policy in Sweden are strongly supported by energetic moral exhortation for women to be self-supporting while producing the next generation of Swedes. The result is a homogeneous culture, in which all institutions and public messages work towards the same goals. Italy achieves the same effect, but with family affairs left far more to families, with little or no public intervention.

Sometimes new trends are the unexpected and unforeseen consequence of intended developments. For example, increasing income inequality between households is the inevitable consequence of rising female employment and the polarisation of women's jobs and careers. Sharp inequalities between no-earner, one-earner, and two-earner households are exacerbated by the decision of some two-earner couples not to have any children, while one-earner and no-earner households often have larger families. Given this long-term increase in income-inequality, poverty must also rise in the long term, given the current focus on *relative* definitions.

More state support for children has its own inevitable consequences, when a husband's financial support is automatically replaced by state support (which is more regular, predictable and reliable than many men are). One-parent families become more viable, divorce becomes less unattractive and financially ruinous. The long-term consequences are shown in Sweden. The consequences of a long-term refusal to improve state support for parents and children are seen in Italy, with its plummeting birth rate.

Sweden has wrapped its pronatalist policies in a 'gender equity' gift wrapping. Based on a combination of feminist claims that all women wanted to combine paid jobs with childrearing, and socialist demands that they should do so, the focus of social policy has been on supporting working mothers—to the extent of decrying full-time mothers. There is good evidence that many women do not want this dual role; instead, they prefer to focus their energies full-time on family work (and large families) or on high-achieving careers (often staying childless to avoid conflicting priorities).[1] It is thus not surprising that recent research has finally shown the pay gap in Sweden to be just as large as elsewhere in Europe,[2] while occupational segregation and the glass ceiling are even greater than in the USA and western Europe.[3] The irony here, as elsewhere, is that lower birth rates can be reversed, but only among the minority of women who are family-centred in their goals and aspirations. Unfortunately, these women are now completely lost from sight in the conventional focus on high-achieving women.

It is finally being recognised that family-friendly policies, even in Sweden, do not eliminate conflicting priorities between work and family, they simply make it more feasible for mothers to do some paid work rather than none.[4] This does not put mothers with (part-time) jobs on the same footing as careerist men in full-time jobs. However, it does curtail their parenting activities. In Italy, mothers face a sharper choice between a full-time homemaker role and full-time employment. But this is not the sole cause of the low fertility rate, which seems to be due rather to a host of problems in combination, including the tendency for children to live at home until their late 20s and 30s.

This, in turn, owes much to a failure to provide fiscal recognition for families that might enable young people to set up home and have children while maintaining some parity in living standards with their childless peers. This failure may be attributable, ironically, to a protective 'hands-off' approach that extends to economic support itself, where the reverence for the family kills the very thing it loves. In the UK, spitefulness towards two-parent families and male breadwinners ensures that birth rates in the middle range of incomes are driven down, while those in more approved mother-only or mother-centric (with men loosely attached) families receive much greater subsidies to form and multiply.

The introduction of reliable modern contraception in the 1960s had several unplanned consequences. Sexual activity became disconnected from marriage and childbearing. Recreational sexual activity increased hugely, and new types of relationship developed around this new popular (but private) pastime. Cohabitation in its current form is a direct result of the contraceptive revolution, and is further extended by large numbers of young people entering higher education. Sexual relationships acquire a contingent character; divorce and separation become acceptable; serial monogamy (or cohabitation) appears. However, policy can restrain or exacerbate these trends. Limiting conditions can be applied to serial partnerships just as much as to marriage, and Sweden's de-familialising policies are not obligatory or inevitable.

The polarisation of women's employment patterns, and of household incomes, point up the need for policies that are more flexible, that cease to rely on the assumption of homogeneity. Cohabitation is also polarised—between the better-educated couples who progress to marriage, and the lower-income, less educated couples whose behaviour can be heavily influenced by welfare benefits, fiscal policy and employment histories. So far, few social scientists, and even fewer policy makers, have recognised the need for analyses that differentiate between polarising groups. Policy will be far more successful if it is based on a correct map of current developments.

It has to be recognised that the relatively low impact of family policies in some countries is due to the lack of consistency and continuity in policy-making. Sweden is an exception here, due to the social and political homogeneity that kept the same political party in power for decades. If Sweden is a model, it is primarily for the consistency and continuity of its social and family policies, which do, eventually, cumulatively, have large impacts. Countries like Italy and France experience changes in government that produce sharp swings in public policy. With no single type of policy dominating, it is not surprising that small bits of tinkering at the edges have little effect. For example, new policies to support full-time mothers and large families alternate with policies to support working women and individualised welfare benefits. One result of the conflicting ideologies and competing policies in western Europe is that many schemes and benefits are in practice non-operational for one reason or another. This is certainly the case in southern Europe, for example.

Labour laws in Italy (as in Spain and Greece) give working women extensive rights to parental leave and other benefits. In practice, these are regarded as so onerous for employers, especially in the context of high unemployment rates, that women do not feel able to take advantage of them.[5] The alternative view is that legislators intentionally gave working women extensive rights so as to ensure that employers would refuse to employ women, forcing them back into the home.[6] In effect, women have to choose between full-time continuous employment (in the same way as men) or full-time homemaking in Italy. This produces a much lower level of employment among women, as noted in Table 1 (p. 7), than in countries (such as Sweden and Britain) where women move flexibly in and out of paid work, and in and out of part-time jobs, over the lifecycle. In turn, another consequence is that working women tend to have no children, or only one child, producing the lowest fertility rate in the EU in the 1990s (see Table 2, pp. 8-10).

While some commentators see policies on the family as a response to family changes, rather than the cause, historically, the fear of falling fertility, if not family decline, have been the most potent catalysts for action. It seems likely that family policy will take centre stage in the foreseeable future.

Notes

1: Introduction

1.   Jonung, C. and Persson, I., 'Women and market work: the misleading tale of participation rates in international comparisons', *Work, Employment and Society*, 1993, 7: 259-274.

2.   Hakim, C., 'The myth of rising female employment', *Work, Employment and Society*, 1993, 7: 97-120; Hakim, C., 'Five feminist myths about women's employment', *British Journal of Sociology*, 1995, 46: 429-455; Hakim, C., *Key Issues in Women's Work*, Cavendish Press, 2004.

3.   Hakim, *Key Issues in Women's Work*, 2004, pp. 133-41.

2: Sweden: Socialist Engineering in Family Policy

1.   Hoem, B. and Hoem, J.M., 'The Disruption of Marital and Nonmarital Unions in Contemporary Sweden', in Trussell, J., Hankinson, R. and Tilton, J. (eds), *'Demographic Applications of Event History Analysis'*, Oxford: Clarendon Press, 1992; and Hoem, J.M., 'The Impact of the First Child on Family Stability', *Stockholm Research Reports in Demography*, 119, Demography Unit, University of Stockholm, 1997.

2.   Gahler, 'Life after Divorce, Economical and psychological well being among Swedish adults and children following family dissolution', 1998.

3.   Kiernan, K., 'Cohabitation in Western Europe', *Population Trends*, 96.

4.   'Population Statistics', European Commission, Luxembourg: Office for Official Publications of the European Communities, 2004.

5.   Kiernan, K., 'European perspectives on non-marital childbearing CASE London School of Economics', Paper for Conference on Non-marital Childbearing, Madison, Wisconsin, 29-30 April 1999.

6.   Kiernan, 'European Perspectives on Non-marital childbearing CASE London School of Economics', 1999.

7.   Nyman, H., 'An economic analysis of lone motherhood in Sweden' (thesis), Goteborg: Department of Economics, Goteborg University, 1998.

8.   Kiernan, 'European perspectives on non-marital childbearing', CASE London School of Economics', 1999.

9.   Carlson, A., *The Swedish Experiment in Family Politics*, New Brunswick, New Jersey: Transaction Pub., 1990, p. xi.

10.   Hakim, C., *Work-Lifestyle Choices in the 21st Century*, Oxford University Press, 2000, p. 237.

11.   Hakim, *Work-Lifestyle Choices in the 21st Century*, 2000, pp. 237-38.

12.   Rojas, M., *Beyond the Welfare State*, the author and AB Timbro, 2001, p. 31.

13.   Lewis, H., *Sweden's Right to be Human*, Allison and Busby Ltd, 1982, p. 3.

14.   Hom Ombudsmannen mot Diskriminering Pa Grund av Sexuell Laggning Rapport 2004 Stockholm p.12.

15.   See Rojas, *Beyond the Welfare State*, 2001.

16.   Rojas, *Beyond the Welfare State*, 2001, p. 31.

17.   Carlson, The Swedish Experiment in Family Politics, 1990.

18.   Quensel, C-E., 'Population Movements in Sweden in Recent Years', *Population Studies*, vol. 1, June 1947, pp. 29-43.

19.   Myrdal, A. & G., *Kris I Befoliningsfragan* (*Crisis in the Population Question*), Stockholm: Bonniers popular edition, 1936; also *Nation and Family: The Swedish Experiment in Democratic Family and Population Policy*, New York: Harper and Brothers, 1941. For a full

exposition of the Myrdals' lives, work and publications see
Carlson, A., *The Swedish Experiment in Family Politics*, London:
Transaction Publishers, 1990.

20.   Carlson, *The Swedish Experiment in Family Politics*, 1990, p. 26.

21.   Carlson, *The Swedish Experiment in Family Politics*, 1990, p. 193.

22.   Carlson, *The Swedish Experiment in Family Politics*, 1990, p. xii.

23.   Lewis, *Sweden's Right to be Human*, 1982, p. 135.

24.   Carlson, *The Swedish Experiment in Family Politics*, 1990, p. 94.
      Quoting Gunnar and Alva Myrdal Kris i befolknigsfragan p. 299.

25.   Lewis, *Sweden's Right to be Human*, 1982, pp. 142-43.

26.   Carlson, *The Swedish Experiment in Family Politics*, 1990.

27.   Carlson, *The Swedish Experiment in Family Politics*, 1990, p. 115.

28.   Incorporated in *Towards Equality: The Alva Myrdal Report to the
      Social Democratic Party*, Stockholm: Prisma, 1971.

29.   Carlson, *The Swedish Experiment in Family Politics*, 1990, p. 201.

30.   See Ginsburg, N., 'Sweden: the Social Democratic Case', in
      Cochrane, A. and Clarke, J., *Comparing Welfare States: Britain in an
      International Context*, London: Sage, 1993.

31.   Report to the Nordic Council of Ministers by an
      intergovernmental committee on sex roles and education,
      reviewed in 1972, Lewis, *Sweden's Right to be Human*, 1982, p. 104.

32.   Bjornberg, U., 'Parenting in Transition: An Introduction and
      Summary', in Bjornberg, U. (ed.), *European Parents in the 1990s*,
      New Jersey: Transaction Books, 1992, p. 12.

33.   Bjornberg, 'Parents' Ideals and Strategies in Sweden', in
      Bjornberg, *European Parents in the 1990s*, 1992, p.86.

34.   Bjornberg, 'Parents' Ideals and Strategies in Sweden', 1992, p. 86.

35.   Bjornberg, U. in Wintersberger, H., 'Work viewed from a childhood perspective' in *Family Observer*, European Commission Luxembourg, 1999.

36.   Abramovici, G., 'Social protection: cash family benefits in Europe', Eurostat European Communities 2003.

37.   Haas, L., *Equal Parenthood and Social Policy: A Study of Parental Leave in Sweden*, Albany, NY: State University of New York Press, 1992.

38.   Haas, *Equal Parenthood and Social Policy: A Study of Parental Leave in Sweden*, 1992.

39.   Meadows, P., *Women at Work in Britain and Sweden*, London: National Institute of Economic and Social Research, 2000.

40.   Ekberg J., Eriksson R. and Friebel G., 'Sharing responsibility? Short and long-term effects of Sweden's daddy-month reform', paper presented to Department of Trade and Industry seminar, 27 May 2004.

41.   Abramovici, 'Social protection: cash family benefits in Europe', Eurostat European Communities, 2003.

42.   *Report of the Committee on One-Parent Families* (The Finer Report), Cmnd 5629, London: HMSO, 1974.

43.   Rosen, S., 'Public Employment and the Welfare State in Sweden', *Journal of Economic Literature*, 34, 1996, pp. 729-40.

44.   Smith, D., 'The Effects of Public Spending and Taxes on Economic Growth', Williams de Broe, 14 May 2004.

45.   *Taxing Wages 2000-2001* OECD publications, Paris, 2001.

46.   *Taxing Wages 2004*, OECD publications, Paris, 2004.

47. Rojas, *Beyond the Welfare State*, 2001, p. 5.

48. Carlson, A.C., 'The Family and the Welfare State', *The St Croix Review*, vol. XXVIII, No. 4, 1995, pp. 21-30.

49. Smith, 'The Effects of Public Spending and Taxes on Economic Growth', Williams de Broe 14 May 2004.

50. Adema, W. *et al*, *Family Policy and the Restructuring of the Welfare State*, Social Policy Division OECD Baruch College, City University of New York, undated.

51. Vogel, J., 'Economic Problems: Living Conditions and Inequality, 1975-1995' (in Swedish with an English summary), in *Levnadsforhallanden*, rapport no.91: Statistics Sweden, 1997.

52. See Joshi, H., *The Cash Opportunity Cost of Childbearing in Britain*, CEPR Discussion Paper, No. 157, 1987; Joshi, H., 'Sex and Motherhood as Handicaps in the Labour Market', in McClean, M. and Groves, D. (eds), *Women's Issues in Social Policy*, London: Routledge, 1991; Davies, H. and Joshi, H., 'Sex, sharing and the distribution of income', Birkbeck Discussion paper, 1992; Ward, C., Joshi, H. and Dales, A., 'Income dependency within couples', National Child Development Study, Working Paper, No. 36, 1993.

53. Burstrom, B. *et al.*, 'Lone mothers in Sweden: trends in health and socio-economic circumstances 1979-1995', *Journal of Epidemiology and Community Health*, 53, 1999, pp. 150-56.

54. Vogel, 'Economic Problems, Living Conditions and Inequality, 1975-1995', in: *Levnadsforhallanden*, 1997.

55. Oxley, H. *et al.*, 'Income Inequalities and Poverty Among Children and Households with Children in Selected OECD Counties: Trends and Determinants', in Vleminckx, K. and Smeeding, T.M. (eds), *Child Well- being, Child Poverty and Child Policy in Modern Nations*, Bristol: The Polity Press, 2000.

56.   Bjornberg and Gardberg, 'Issues Concerning the Family in Sweden in 1996', 1998.

57.   Bjornberg, U., 'Sweden: Supported Workers who Mother', in Duncan, S. and Edwards, R., *Single Mothers in an International Context: Mothers or Workers?*, London: UCL Press, 1997.

58.   Weitoft, G.R, Haglund, B. and Rosen, M., 'Mortality among lone mothers in Sweden: a population study', *Lancet*, vol. 355, 8 April 2000, pp. 1215-219.

59.   Nyman, H., 'An Economic Analysis of Lone Motherhood in Sweden', (thesis) Goteborg: Department of Economics, Goteborg University, 1998.

60.   Bjornberg, 'Sweden: Supported Workers who Mother', in Duncan and Edwards, *Single Mothers in an International Context: Mothers or Workers?* 1997, p. 263.

61.   Bjornberg, 'Sweden: Supported Workers who Mother', 1997.

62.   Sweden's Action Plan against Poverty and Social Exclusion Stockholm: Government Offices of Sweden, 2003.

63.   Gahler, M., 'Life after Divorce: Economical and psychological well being among Swedish adults and children following family dissolution', Dissertation series 32 (thesis), Stockholm: Swedish Institute for Social Research, 1998.

64.   Gahler, 'Life after divorce; Economical and psychological well being among Swedish adults and children following family dissolution', 1998.

65.   Ginsburg, N., 'Sweden: The Social Democratic Case', in Cochrane, A. and Clarke, J., *Comparing Welfare States: Britain in an International Context*, London: Sage, 1993.

66.   Bjornberg, 'Sweden: Supported Workers who Mother', 1997, p. 249.

67.   Sweden's Action Plan against Poverty and Social Exclusion, Stockholm: Government Offices of Sweden, 2003.

68.   Gahler, 'Life after Divorce: Economical and psychological well being among Swedish adults and children following family dissolution', 1998.

69.   Svedin, C.G. and Wadsby, M., 'The Presence of Psychiatric Consultations in Relation to Divorce', *Acta Psychiatrica Scandinavica* 98 (5) pp. 414-22.

70.   Burstrom, B. *et al.*, 'Lone Mothers in Sweden: Trends in Health and Socio-economic Circumstances, 1979-1995', *J Epidemiol Community Health*, 53, 1999, pp. 150-56.

71.   Bjornberg, 'Sweden: Supported Workers who Mother', 1997, p. 249.

72.   Gahler, 'Life after Divorce: Economical and psychological well being among Swedish adults and children following family dissolution', 1998.

73.   Hope, S., Power, C. and Rodgers, B., 'Does Financial Hardship Account for Elevated Psychological Distress in Lone Mothers?' *Social Science and Medicine*, 49, 1999, pp. 1637-649.

74.   Gahler, 'Life after Divorce: Economical and psychological well being among Swedish adults and children following family dissolution', 1998.

75.   Whitehead, M. *et al.*, 'Social Policies and the Pathways to Inequalities in Health: A Comparative Analysis of Lone Mothers in Britain and Sweden', *Social Science and Medicine*, 50, 2000, pp. 255-70.

76.   Burstrom *et al.*, 'Lone Mothers in Sweden: Trends in Health and Socio-economic Circumstances, 1979-1995', 1999.

77.   Vogel, J., 'Economic Problems. Living Conditions and Inequality,
       1975-1995' (in Swedish with an English summary), in:
       Levnadsforhallanden, rapport no.91, Statistics Sweden, 1997.

78.   Rsengren, A., Wedel, H. and Wilhemsen, L., 'Marital Status and
       Mortality in Middle-aged Swedish Men', *American Journal of
       Epidemiology*, 129, pp. 54-64.

79.   Weitoft, G.R, Haglund, B. and Rosen, M., 'Mortality Among Lone
       Mothers in Sweden: A Population Study', *Lancet*, Vol. 355, 8 April
       2000, pp. 1215-219.

80.   Sweden's Action Plan against Poverty and Social Exclusion,
       Stockholm: Government Offices of Sweden, 2003.

81.   Whitehead *et al.*, 'Social Policies and the Pathways to Inequalities
       in Health: A Comparative Analysis of Lone Mothers in Britain
       and Sweden', 2000, p. 266.

82.   Duncan, S. and Edwards, R., *Lone Mothers, Paid Work and
       Gendered Moral Rationalities*, Basingstoke: Macmillan Press Ltd,
       1999, p. 34.

83.   Ringback Weitoft, G., 'Mortality, Severe Morbidity, and Injury in
       Children Living with Single Parents in Sweden: A Population
       Based Study', *Lancet*, Vol. 361, No. 9354, 25 January 2003.

84.   Unicef, A League Table of Child Maltreatment Deaths in Rich
       Nations, Innocenti Report Card, Issue no. 5, 2003.

85.   'A Reasonable Approach to Discipline: Issues to be considered in
       the Context of the Debate on Parental Smacking', Twickenham:
       Family Education Trust, October 2004.

86.   Larzelere, R.E., *Sweden's Smacking Ban: More Harm than Good*,
       Christian Institute and Families First, 2004.

87.   Ringback Weitoft, 'Mortality, Severe Morbidity, and Injury in
       Children Living with Single Parents in Sweden: A Population
       Based Study', 2003.

88. Jonsson, J.O. and Gahler, M ., 'Family Dissolution, Family
     Reconstruction, and Children's Educational Careers: Recent
     Evidence from Sweden', *Demography*, Vol. 34, No. 2, 1997, pp.
     277-93.

89. Gahler, M., 'Parental Divorce in Childhood and Demographic
     Transitions in Early Adulthood: Evidence for Sweden', MIMEO
     Stockholm: Swedish Institute for Social Research, 1997.

90. Kiernan, K., 'Cohabitation in Western Europe', *Population Trends*
     96.

91. Stattin, H. and Magnusson, C., 'Behavioural and interpersonal
     antecedents behind the age of leaving home and the future
     consequences for parent-child relations', 1994 paper presented at
     the biannual meetings of the Society for Research on
     Adolescence, San Diego. See Steinberg, L., *Adolescence*, New York:
     MaGraw Hill Inc., 1996 .

92. Aquilino, W.S., 'Family Structure and Home Leaving: A Further
     Specification of the Relationship', *Journal of Marriage and the
     Family*, No. 53, 1991, pp. 999-1,010.

93. Dunn, J. and Deater-Deckard, K., *Children's Views of their
     Changing Families*, York: Joseph Rowntree Foundation, 2001.

94. Ferri, E., *Step Children*, Windsor: NFER-Nelson, 1984. Also see
     Hobcraft, J., 'Intergenerational and Life-Course Transmission of
     Social Exclusion: Influences of Childhood Poverty, Family
     Disruption, and Contact with the Police', CASEpaper 15,
     STICERD Centre for Analysis of Social Exclusion, London:
     London School of Economics, 1998; Kim, J.E., Hetherington, E.M.
     and Reiss, D., 'Associations among Family Relationships,
     Antisocial Peers, and Adolescents' Externalising Behaviours:
     Gender and Family Type Differences', *Child Development*, Vol. 70,
     No. 5, 1999, pp. 1209-230.

95. Amato, P.R. and Booth, A., 'Consequences of Parental Divorce
     and Marital Unhappiness for Adult Well Being', *Social Forces*,
     Vol. 69, 1991, pp. 895-914.

96.   Gahler, 'Life after Divorce: Economical and psychological well
        being among Swedish adults and children following family
        dissolution', 1998; and Lundberg, O., 'The Impact of Childhood
        Living Conditions on Illness and Mortality in Adulthood', *Social
        Science and Medicine*, Vol. 36, 1993, pp. 1047-052.

97.   Schwartz, J.E. *et al.*, 'Sociodemographic and Psychosocial Factors
        in Childhood as Predictors of Adult Mortality', *American Journal
        of Public Health*, Vol. 85, 1995, pp. 1237-245.

98.   Tucker, J.S. *et al.*, 'Parental Divorce: Effects on Individual
        Behaviour and Longevity', *Journal of Personality and Social
        Psychology*, 73, 1997, pp. 381-91.

99.   Singh, G.K. and Yu, S.M., 'US Childhood Mortality, 1950 through
        1993: Trends and Socioeconomic Differentials', *American Journal
        of Public Health*, Vol. 85, No. 4, 1995, pp. 505-12.

100.   Nyman, H., 'An economic analysis of lone motherhood in
        Sweden' (thesis), Goteborg: Department of Economics, Goteborg
        University, 1998.

101.   Popenoe, D., 'Beyond the Nuclear Family: A Statistical Portrait of
        the Changing Family in Sweden', *Journal of Marriage and the
        Family*, 49, 1987, pp. 173-183.

102.   Melkas, H. and Anker, R., 'Occupational segregation by sex in
        Nordic countries: An empirical investigation', *International Labour
        Review*, 136, 1997, pp. 341-360.

103.   Hakim, C., *Work-Lifestyle Choices in the 21st Century*, Oxford
        University Press, 2000, p. 241.

104.   Hakim, C., *Key Issues in Women's Work*, Glasshouse, 2004, pp. 171,
        183.

107.   Hakim, *Key Issues in Women's Work*, 2004, p. 178; see also
        Albrecht, J., Bjorklund, A. and Vroman, S., 'Is there a glass ceiling
        in Sweden?', *Journal of Labor Economics*, 21, 2003, pp. 145-77.

106. Hakim, *Work-Lifestyle Choices in the 21st Century*, 2000, pp. 116, 240; Hakim, *Key Issues in Women's Work*, 2004, pp. 171-73, 178-82.

107. Hakim, *Work-Lifestyle Choices in the 21st Century*, 2000, p. 5.

108. Esping-Andersen, G., *The Three Worlds of Welfare Capitalism*, Cambridge: Polity Press 1990, p. 156.

109. Lewis, *Sweden's Right to be Human*, 982, p. 78.

110. Bergstrom, R., 'Labour Reform Needed to Sustain Costly Swedish Welfare System', *Financial Times*, 10 June 2005.

111. Einhorn, B., *Cinderella Goes to Market: Citizenship, Gender and Women's Movements in East Central Europe*, London: Verso, 1993.

112. Lamb, M.E., *et al.*, 'Determinants of Social Competence in Swedish Pre-schoolers', *Developmental Psychology*, Vol. 24, No. 1, 1988, pp.58-70; also see Cochran, M., 'A Comparison of Group Daycare and Family Childrearing Patterns in Sweden', *Child Development*, Vol. 48, 1977, pp.702-07.

113. Haas, L., 'Equal Parenthood and Social Policy: Lessons from a Study of Parental Leave in Sweden', in Hyde, J.S. and Essex, M.J. (eds), *Parental Leave and Child Care*, Temple University Press, 1991.

114. Hoem, J.M., 'Social Policy and Recent Fertility Change in Sweden', *Population and Development Review*, December 1990.

115. Bjornberg, 'Sweden: Supported Workers who Mother', 1997.

116. Haas, L., *Equal Parenthood and Social Policy: A Study of Parental Leave in Sweden*, Albany, NY: State University of New York Press, 1992.

117. Haas, 'Equal Parenthood and Social Policy: Lessons from a Study of Parental Leave in Sweden', 1991.

118. Hakim, *Key Issues in Women's Work*, 2004, p. 185.

119. Lewis, *Sweden's Right to be Human*, 1982, p. 72.

120. Lewis, *Sweden's Right to be Human*, 1982, p. 77.

121. Lewis, *Sweden's Right to be Human*, 1982, pp. 147-48.

122. Vogel, 'Economic Problems, Living conditions and inequality, 1975-1995', 1997.

123. Lewis, H., *Sweden's Right to be Human*, Allison and Busby Ltd, 1982, p. 70.

124. Rojas, *Beyond the Welfare State*, 2001.

125. Austrian Institute of Family Studies, 1998, quoted in *Family Observer*, European Communities Luxembourg 3, 2001.

3: Italy: Hotel Mama is Closing Down

1. European Commission, 'The Demographic Situation in the European Union', Directorate General V, Brussels, 1996, pp. 48-49.

2. Kiernan, 'Cohabitation in Western Europe' *Population Trends*, 96.

3. Kiernan, K., 'European perspectives on Non-marital Childbearing', CASE London School of Economics, paper for conference on non-marital childbearing, Madison, Wisconsin, 29-30 April 1999.

4. Kiernan, 'Cohabitation in Western Europe', *Population Trends*, 96.

5. Parris, M., 'Sweep out religious superstition that will not tolerate me', *The Times*, 23 October 2004.

6. Palmoba, R., 'Postponement in family formation in Italy, within the southern European context', Institute for Population Research, Rome. Paper presented at IUSSP Seminar on International Perspectives on Low Fertility: Trends, Theories and Policies, Tokyo, Japan, March 2001.

7. Sgritta, G.B. and Zanatta, A.L., 'Families and Family Policy in Italy: Constraints and Promises', in Dumon, W. (ed.), *Changing Family Policies in the Member States of the European Union*, European Observatory on National Family Policies, 1994, p. 179.

8. Cuyvers, P. and Kalle, P., *Caring for the Next Generation: Family Life Cycle, Income and Fertility Decisions*, Netherlands Family Council Study Series, 2002, p. 11.

9. Ingelhart, R., *Modernization and Postmodernization: Cultural, Economic and Political Change in 43 Societies*, Princeton, NJ: Princeton University Press, 1997.

10. Cuyvers and Kalle, *Caring for the Next Generation: Family Life Cycle, Income and Fertility Decisions*, 2002.

11. Eurostat, *Education in the EU*, Report No. 9/98, Luxembourg: OOPEC, 1998.

12. Lichter, D.T. *et al.*, 'Race and the Retreat from Marriage: A Shortage of Marriageable Men?', *American Sociological Review*, 57, 1992, pp. 781-99.

13. Grossbard-Shechtman, S., *On the Economics of Marriage: A Theory of Marriage, Labor and Divorce*, Boulder, Colorado: Westview Press, 1993.

14. Bagavos, C. and Martin, C., *Low Fertility, Families and Public Policies*, Synthesis Report No.10, European Observatory on Family Matters, Austrian Institute for Family Studies, 2000.

15. Sgritta, G.B., 'Family and Welfare Systems in the Transition to Adulthood: An Emblematic Case Study', in Chisholm, L. (ed.), *Family Forms and the Young Generation in Europe*, European Observatory on Family Matters, 16, Milan, 2001.

16. Di Tommaso, M.L., 'A Trivariate Model of Participation, Fertility and Wages: The Italian Case', *Cambridge Journal of Economics*, 23, 1999, pp. 623-40.

17.   O'Donoghue, C. and Sutherland, H., 'Accounting for the Family in European Income Tax Systems', *Cambridge Journal of Economics*, 23, 1999, pp. 565-98.

18.   Gonzalez, L., 'The Determinants of the Prevalence of Single Mothers: A Cross Country Analysis', Northwestern University, unpublished, 2003.

19.   Hoogervorst, H., 'Welfare Reform', in *Europe's Welfare Burden: The Case for Reform*, London: Civitas, 2002.

20.   Thomson, D., 'Cohort Fortunes and Demographic Change in the Twentieth Century', Working Paper Series: No.6, Cambridge Group for the History of Population and Social Structure, Cambridge, 1998; and Thomson, D., *Selfish Generations*, Wellington: Bridget Williams Books, 1991.

21.   Thomson, *Selfish Generations*, 1991, p. 193.

22.   Thomson, *Selfish Generations*, 1991, p. 206.

23.   Bagavos, C. and Martin, C., 'Low Fertility, Families and Public Policies', Synthesis Report No.10, European Observatory on Family Matters, Austrian Institute for Family Studies, 2000, quoting Massimo Livi-Bacci in *New York Times*, 10 July 1998, p. 28.

24.   Manacorda, M. and Moretti, E., 'Why do Most Italian Young Men Live with Their Parents? Intergenerational Transfers and Household Structure', London: Centre for Economic Policy Research, 2005.

25.   Bagavos and Martin, 'Low Fertility, Families and Public Policies', 2000, quoting Massimo Livi-Bacci, in *New York Times*, 10 July1998, p. 28.

26.   Sgritta, G.B., 'Italy: The Year of the Family?', in Ditch, J., Barnes, H. and Bradshaw, J., *Developments in National Family Policies in 1995*, European Observatory on National Family Policies, University of York, 1996. p. 86.

27.   Sgritta, 'Italy: The Year of the Family?', 1996, p. 88.

28.   Sgritta, G.B., 'European citizenship?' in *Family Observer*,
       European Observatory on Family Matters, European
       Commission, No. 2, 2000.

29.   Sgritta, G.B. and Zanatta, A.L., 'Families and Family Policy in
       Italy: Constraints and Promises', in Dumon, W. (ed.), *Changing
       Family Policies in the Member States of the European Union*,
       European Observatory on National Family Policies, 1994, p. 186.

30.   Sgritta and Zanatta, 'Families and Family Policy in Italy:
       Constraints and Promises', 1994, p. 189.

31.   Sgritta and Zanatta, 'Italy', 1998, p. 138.

32.   Ditch, J.A. *et al.*, *Synthesis of National Family Policies 1996*,
       European Observatory on National Family Policies, University of
       York: European Commission, 1998.

33.   Oxley, H. *et al.*, 'Income Inequalities and Poverty Among
       Children and Households with Children in Selected OECD
       Countries: Trends and Determinants', in Vleminckx, K. and
       Smeeding, T.M. (eds), *Child Well being, Child Poverty and Child
       Policy in Modern Nations*, Bristol: The Polity Press, 2000.

34.   Atella, V., Coromaldi, M. and Mastrofrancesco, L., 'Italy',
       Euromod Country Reports, University of Rome, 2001.

35.   Eurostat, *Digest of Statistics on Social Protection in Europe*, vol. IV,
       Luxembourg, 1993, pp. 70-71.

36.   *Taxing Wages 2000-2001*, Paris: OECD, 2002.

37.   Sgritta, 'Italy: The Year of the Family?', in *Developments in
       National Family Policies in 1995*, 1996.

38.   O'Donoghue, C. and Sutherland, H., 'Accounting for the Family
       in European Income Tax Systems', *Cambridge Journal of Economics*,
       23, 1999, pp. 565-98.

39. Abramovici, G., *Social Protection: Cash Family Benefits in Europe*, Eurostat European Communities, 2003.

40. Sgritta, G.B., 'Family and Welfare Systems in the Transition to Adulthood: An Emblematic Case Study', in Chisholm, L. (ed.), *Family Forms and the Young Generation in Europe*, European Observatory on Family Matters, 16, Milan 2001; and Willem, A. *et al.*, 'Family Policy and the Restructuring of the Welfare State: A Comparative Analysis of OEDC Countries', unpublished paper Social Policy Division Baruch College, New York.

41. *Taxing Wages 2003-2004*, OECD, 2004.

42. Ditch *et al.*, *Synthesis of National Family Policies 1996*, 1998; and *Taxing Wages 2000-2001*, Paris: OECD publications, 2001.

43. Mingione, E., 'Urban Poverty in the Advanced Industrial World: Concepts, Analysis, and Debates', in Mingione, E. (ed.), *Urban Poverty and the Underclass*, Oxford: Basil Blackwell, 1996.

44. Sgritta, G.B., 'Family and Welfare Systems in the Transition to Adulthood: Am Emblematic Case Study', European Observatory on Family Matters, 16, 2003, p. 79.

45. Bagavos and Martin, 'Low Fertility, Families and Public Policies', 2000, p. 22.

46. Cordon, J.A.F., 'Low Fertility as an Issue for Social Policy', paper for the Annual Seminar 2004, *Europe's Coming Generations*, European Observatory on the Social Situation, Demography and Family, Brussels, 27-28 September 2004.

47. Bagavos and Martin, 'Low Fertility, Families and Public Policies', 2000, p. 22.

48. Bagavos and Martin, 'Low Fertility, Families and Public Policies', 2000, p. 15.

49.   Sgritta, G.B., 'European Citizenship?', in *Family Observer*,
        European Observatory on Family Matters European
        Commission, No. 2, 2000.

50.   Bagavos and Martin, 'Low Fertility, Families and Public Policies',
        2000, pp. 14-15.

51.   Bagavos and Martin, 'Low Fertility, Families and Public Policies',
        2000, p. 17.

52.   Bagavos and Martin, 'Low Fertility, Families and Public Policies',
        2000, p. 23.

4: Britain: the Worst of All Worlds?

1.   Statistics drawn from Berthoud, R. and Gershuny, J., *Seven Years
        in the Lives of British Families*, University of Essex ESRC 2000,
        based on the General Household Survey; *Social Focus on Men*,
        National Statistics: the Stationery Office, 2001; 'Living in Britain
        2001', from General Household Survey.

2.   Berger, P. and Berger, B., *The War Over the Family*, London:
        Hutchinson & Co., 1983.

3.   Minutes of Evidence, *Royal Commission on Marriage and Divorce
        1955 (The Morton Commission)*, Evidence from The Ethical Union,
        29th day, p. 765.

4.   Duncan Smith, I., 'Why I'm Backing Bush', *Spectator*, 18
        September 2004.

5.   Williams, F., *Rethinking Families*, London: Calouste Gulbenkian
        Foundation, 2004, p. 11.

6.   Wootton, B., 'Holiness or Happiness', *Twentieth Century*,
        November 1955, p. 407.

7.   McGregor, O.R., *Divorce in England*, Heinemann, 1957, p. 161.

8.   McGregor, *Divorce in England*, 1957, p. 167.

9.   McGregor, *Divorce in England*, 1957.

10.   Deech, R., *Divorce Dissent: Dangers in Divorce Reform*, London: Centre for Policy Studies, 1994, p. 10.

11.   McGregor, *Divorce in England*, 1957, p. 152.

12.   *Looking to the Future: Mediation and the Ground for Divorce*, Lord Chancellor's Department, Cm 2799, London: HMSO, 1995.

13.   *Report of the Committee on One-Parent Families*, Lord Chancellor's Department, Cmnd 5629, London: HMSO, 1974.

14.   *Report of the Committee on One-Parent Families*, Cmnd 5629, 1974, para. 4.224.

15.   *Report of the Committee on One-Parent Families*, Cmnd 5629, 1974, para. 4.49.

16.   McGregor, *Divorce in England*, 1957, p. 199.

17.   *The Report of the Committee on One Parent Families (The Finer Report)*, vol. 1, London: HMSO, 1974, pp. 295-96.

18.   'Households Below Average Income 1979-1996/7', Department of Social Security, 1998; see also Giles, C. and Webb, S., *Poverty Statistics: A Guide for the Perplexed*, London: Institute for Fiscal Studies, 1993; and Roll, J., *Understanding Poverty*, Occasional Paper, No. 15, London: Family Policy Studies Centre, 1992.

19.   Barclay, P. (chair), *Income and Wealth*, Vol. 1: Report of the Enquiry Group; and Hills, J., *A Summary of the Evidence: Joseph Rowntree Foundation Inquiry into Income and Wealth*, Vol. 2, York: Rowntree Foundation, 1995 & 1998. Between 1987-98, the share of income by the top 20 per cent was 46.9 per cent and for the poorest 20 per cent it was 2.7 per cent. *Human Development Report 2000*, United Nations Development Program, Oxford: Oxford University Press, 2000. For the poorer 80 per cent of the

population, the share of national gross income steadily declined over the period 1983/4 -1995/6, the richer five and ten per cents saw a marked increase. Podder, N. and Chatterjee, S., *Sharing the National Cake in Post Reform New Zealand: Income Inequality Trends in Terms of Income Sources*, paper presented at the Annual Conference of the New Zealand Association of Economists, Wellington, 2-4 September 1998.

20. The share of equivalent income of those in the bottom and top 20 per cents grew between the mid-1980s and mid-1990s, while there were real falls for the middle 40 per cent. Harding, A., *Emerging Trends in Income Inequality in Australia 1982 to 1993/4*, Australian Population Association, Eighth National Conference, University of Canberra, 6 December 1996.

21. Hills, *A Summary of the Evidence: Joseph Rowntree Foundation Inquiry into Income and Wealth*, Vol. 2, 1995 &1998.

22. Hills, J., *Inquiry into Income and Wealth: A Summary of the Evidence*, Vol. 2, York: Joseph Rowntree Foundation, 1995. In 1979, only four per cent of UK couples with only one person in full-time work were below the poverty threshold, but in 1995/6 this had risen to 18 per cent. Warin, J. *et al.*, *Fathers, Work and Family Life*, London: Family Policy Studies Centre, 1999.

23. Hakim, C., 'Models of the Family, Women's Role and Social Policy: A New Perspective from Preference Theory', *European Societies*, 1(1), 1999, pp. 33-58.

24. Hills, *Inquiry into Income and Wealth: A Summary of the Evidence*, Vol. 2, 1995.

25. *Households Below Average Income 1999/2000*, DSS publications: 2001.

26. *Households Below Average Income 1979-1996/7*, Department of Social Security, Government Statistical Service, 1998; and *Households Below Average Income 1999/00*, Department of Social Security, Government Statistical Service, 2001.

27. Shouls, S. *et al*, 'The Health and Socioeconomic Status of British Lone Mothers Over the Last Two Decades', *Population Trends 95*, 1999, pp. 41-46.

28. Shouls *et al.*, 'The Health and Socioeconomic Status of British Lone Mothers Over the Last Two Decades', 1999, pp. 41-46.

29. 'Non-resident Fathers in Britain', *Research Results*, ESRC Population and Household Change Research Programme, No. 14, 1999.

30. 'A League Table of Child Poverty in Rich Nations', June 2000.

31. From 1975 to 1993, the proportion of UK two-adult households where both worked rose from 51 to 60 per cent, but the proportion with no earner increased from three to 11 per cent. Gregg, P., Harkness, S. and Machin, S., *Child Development and Family Income*, York: Joseph Rowntree Foundation, 1999; and Hills, *Inquiry into Income and Wealth: A Summary of the Evidence*, vol. 2, 1995.

32. 'Labour Force Survey 1998', in *Labour Market Trends*, 1999, ONS, The Stationery Office. Less than two-thirds of children in workless families were in low income households in 1979, but by 1995/6, almost all children in workless UK families were in households with less than half average income.

33. McKay, S., Walker, R. and Youngs, R., *Unemployment and Jobseeking before Jobseeker's Allowance*, DSS Research Report, No. 73, London: Stationery Office, 1997.

34. Hakim, C., *Models of the Family in Modern Societies: Ideals and Realities*, Aldershot: Ashgate, 2003, p. 226.

35. Field, F., *Poverty and Politics*,Oxford: Heinemann, 1982, p. 1936.

36 Field, *Poverty and Politics*, 1982.

37. *Hansard*, cols. 589-90, 5 November 1993; and *Hansard*, cols. 219-20, 8 February 1994.

38. Barnes, M. *et al.*, 'Families and Children in Britain: Findings from the 2003 Families and Children Study', DWP Research Report, 250, 2005.

39. Adam, S. and Brewer, M., *Supporting Families: The Financial Costs and Benefits of Children Since 1975*, The Polity Press for the Joseph Rowntree Foundation, 2004; also Adam, S., Brewer, M. and Reed, H., *The Benefits of Parenting: Government Financial Support for Families with Children since 1975*, Institute for Fiscal Studies, Commentary 90, 2002.

40. *Social Trends 30*, ONS Stationery Office, 2000.

41. FACS, 2002, p. 4.

42. Green, H. *et al.*, *Housing in England 1997-98*, London: The Stationery Office, 1999.

43. Millar, J., Webb, S. and Kemp, M., *Combining Work and Welfare*, York: Joseph Rowntree Foundation, 1997; and Marsh, A. and McKay, S., *Families, Work and Benefits*, London: Policy Studies Institute, 1993.

44. Marsh, A., 'Lowering the Barriers to Work in Britain', *Social Policy Journal New Zealand*, Issue 8, March 1997.

45. *The Battle Against Exclusion*, Paris: OECD Publications, 1998; see also Finn, D., 'Job Guarantees for the Unemployed: Lessons from Australian Welfare Reform', *Journal of Social Policy*, Vol. 28, 1999, pp. 53-71.

46. Riches, V., *Who Cares for Children?* Family and Youth Concern, 1989.

47. Smart, C., *The Ties that Bind*, Routledge and Kegan Paul, 1984, p. 225.

48. I have paraphrased Kreeft, P., *Boston College Observer*, Vol. 16, No. 12, April 2004.

49.   'Responses to Civil Partnerships: A Framework for the Legal Recognition of Same Sex Couples', Women and Equality Unit, 2003, p. 44.

50.   Smart, C., 'The Changing Status of Marriage in Family Law', paper for NPFI and One Plus One Seminar, 31 January 2001.

51.   Kiernan, K., 'Cohabitation and Divorce across Nations and Generations', CASEpaper 65, Centre for Analysis of Social Exclusion, 2003, p. 29.

52.   Kamerman, S.B. and Kahn, A.J., *Family Change and Family Policies in Great Britain, Canada, New Zealand, and the United States,* Oxford: Clarendon Press, 1997, p. 25.

53.   Piachaud, D. and Sutherland, H., 'Changing Poverty Post-1997', CASEpaper 63, Centre for Analysis of Social Exclusion, London School of Economics, 2002; and Brewer, M. *et al., Poverty and Inequality in Britain: 2004,* Institute of Fiscal Studies, 2004; also Brewer, M., Clark, T. and Goodman, A., *The Government's Child Poverty Target: How Much Progress Has Been Made?* Commentary No. 88, London: Institute for Fiscal Studies, 2002.

54.   Brewer *et al., Poverty and Inequality in Britain: 2004,* 2004; and Brewer, M. *et al., Poverty and Inequality in Britain: 2005,* Institute of Fiscal Studies, 2005.

55.   Barnes *et al.,* 'Families and Children in Britain: Findings from the 2003 Families and Children Study', 2005; also see Brewer *et al., Poverty and Inequality in Britain: 2005,* 2005.

56.   Francesconi, M. and Van der Klaauw, W., 'The Consequences of "In Work" Benefit Reform in Britain: New Evidence from Panel Data', ISER Working Papers, No. 2004-13.

57.   Mead, L.M., *The New Paternalism: Supervisory Approaches to Poverty,* Washington DC: Brookings, 1997.

58.   Mead, L.M., 'Welfare Reform and the Family', *Family Matters,* No. 54, Spring/Summer 1999,

59. *The Battle Against Exclusion*, 1998; see also Finn, D., 'Job Guarantees for the Unemployed: Lessons from Australian Welfare Reform', *Journal of Social Policy*, Vol. 28, 1999, pp. 53-71.

60. Hales, J. *et al.*, 'Evaluation of the New Deal for Lone Parent: Early Lessons from the Phase One Prototype', DWP Research Report, 108, 2004.

61. Marsh, A., 'Making It Work for Lone Parents', *Guardian*, 31 December 1997.

62. Brewer *et al.*, *Poverty and Inequality in Britain: 2004*, 2004.

63. 'The Speech: Gordon Brown', *The Times*, 3 December 2004.

64. 'Choice for Parents, the Best Start for Children: A Ten Year Strategy for Childcare', HM Treasury, December 2004.

65. Mayer, S.E., *What Money Can't Buy*, Cambridge, Mass: Harvard University Press, 1997.

66. Ermisch, J., Francesconi, M. and Pevalin, D.J., 'Childhood Parental Behaviour and Young People's Outcomes', ISER University of Essex, 2002.

67. '"Nanny State" Minister Under Fire', *BBC News Online*, 26 November 2004.

68. Baskerville, S., *The Fatherhood Crisis: Time for a New Look*, National Centre for Policy Analysis, Report No. 267, June 2004.

5: Overview and Conclusions

1. Hakim, C., *Work-Lifestyle Choices in the 21st Century: Preference Theory*, Oxford University Press, 2000; Hakim, C., *Models of the Family in Modern Societies: Ideals and Realities*, Ashgate, 2003; Hakim, C., 'A New Approach to Explaining Fertility Patterns: Preference Theory', *Population and Development Review*, 29, 2003, pp. 349-74.

2.   Hakim, *Work-Lifestyle Choices in the 21st Century*, 2000, p. 171.

3.   Hakim, C., *Key Issues in Women's Work*, Cavendish/Glasshouse, 2004, pp. 170-82.

4.   Charles, M. and Grusky, D.B., *Occupational Ghettos*, Stanford, CA: Stanford University Press, 2004; Hakim, *Key Issues in Women's Work*, 2004; Jacobs, J.A. and Gerson, K., *The Time Divide: Work, Family and Gender Inequality*, Cambridge, MA: Harvard University Press, 2004.

5.   Hantrais, L., *Gendered Policies in Europe: Reconciling Employment and Family Life*, Basingstoke: Macmillan, 2000, pp. 108-23.

6.   Hantrais, *Gender Policies in Europe*, 2000, pp. 112-13.